NAKED IN A
PYRAMID

NAKED IN A PYRAMID

Travels & Observations

YOSEF WOSK

anvil
PRESS

Anvil Press • Vancouver

Library and Archives Canada Cataloguing in Publication

Title: Naked in a pyramid : (travels and observations) / Yosef Wosk.
Names: Wosk, Yosef, author.
Description: First edition. | Includes bibliographical references.
Identifiers: Canadiana 20230460879 | ISBN 9781772142204 (softcover)
Subjects: LCGFT: Essays.
Classification: LCC PS8645.O85 N35 2023 | DDC C814/.6—dc23

Editor: Alan Twigg
Cover photo by Joshua Berson
Book design: Get To The Point
Represented in Canada by Publishers Group Canada
Distributed by Raincoast Books

The publisher gratefully acknowledges the financial assistance of the Canada Council for the Arts,
the Canada Book Fund, and the Province of British Columbia through the BC Arts Council and
the Book Publishing Tax Credit.

Anvil Press Publishers Inc.
P.O. Box 3008, Station Terminal
Vancouver, B.C. V6B 3X5 Canada
www.anvilpress.com

PRINTED AND BOUND IN CANADA

"I partnered the earth,
took the planet in my arms and
danced with eternity."

— Y.W.

CONTENTS

FOREWORD

LIKE THAT CLASSIC FOOL IN THE TAROT with his belongings suspended on a pole, I have often set off from family and safety, lured by the notion of wisdom, to seek new fields of opportunity. Travel, for me, has always been a necessary devotion. Tempted by extravagant destinations, I still leave some things to chance. That is where one is most likely to meet the accidental angel inviting one to partake in unexpected revelation.

I have always wanted to reach the highest or most iconic spots. There is something about these high elevations that symbolize removing oneself from the mundane and moving towards transcendence, either to gods or ultimate reality. Among the most exceptional sites I've visited were the six Greek Orthodox monasteries of bell-laden Meteora, a name that translates as "suspended in the air." At that mystic place—perched atop some of the most inaccessible rock formations on the planet—I marvelled for three days and into the darkest of nights at how those precarious monasteries clung to the landscape like clouds to the sky. Monks have prayed in the nearby caves in central Greece since the fourteenth century.

In Bhutan—a tranquil country that issues a limited number of tourist visas per year—we trekked through rugged mountain forests for hours before coming face to face with the remote Tiger's Nest, a stunning Himalayan Buddhist temple complex, established in 1692. It is here that Guru Padmasambhava is believed to have meditated at its Taktsang Senge Samdup cave for four high-altitudinous months, back in the eighth century. Legend has it that he was carried up the cliffside on the back of a tigress.

In China, my Tibetan guide and I, aided by our bamboo walking sticks, followed lush woodland paths like apparitions through the mist and climbed thousands of steps up Mount Emei, the tallest of the Four Sacred Mountains in China. They were venerated by followers of the Tao even before the advent of Buddhism in the country. Some hours later— after encountering waterfalls, swift flowing rivers, forest-dwelling monkeys, and stopping for refreshments at a small village eatery on the side of the road—we reached the principal monastery atop the cloud-enshrouded peak where we meditated at the country's first Buddhist temple, built in the first century BCE.

Some elevations can be disorienting. Quito (9,350 feet above sea level in Ecuador) and Lhasa (12,000 feet above sea level in Tibet) literally took my breath away. Due to lower levels of oxygen, their altitudes gave me headaches and made me lethargic for days. I kept asking myself: "Who turned up the gravity?"

In Lhasa, I nonetheless trudged up the steep hill to enter the chimerical Potala Palace where the interior was illuminated by ghee lamps— clarified yak butter in bowls with floating wicks. In Tibetan Buddhist tradition, the proliferation of burning candles or lamps is conducive for meditation and focusing the mind. It represents enlightenment. The lamps produce a slightly smokey, moody light that results in a heightened spiritual glow. According to the Root Tantra of Chakrasamvara, "If you wish for sublime realization, offer hundreds of lights." So, in an effort to banish darkness, monks and lay people alike kindle thousands of lamps on important holidays in the highest palace in the world, in the centre of the Tibetan Plateau, just north of the Himalayan mountains. These lamps are placed on scaffolds that may be several storeys high. Tibetan devotees supply the ghee butter and vegetable oil to the monasteries to gain merit. Just as matter—in the form of butter or oil—turns into illumination, so it is believed that negativity in human consciousness can analogously be transformed into enlightenment.

The thirteen storeys of buildings in centuries-old Potala Palace contain over 1,000 rooms, 10,000 shrines and 200,000 iconic statues. I became lost amid a maze of passageways and rooms filled with ritual objects and sacred scrolls as pilgrims alternately walked and prostrated themselves on their journeys toward spiritual fulfilment. Nearby was Jokhang Temple, a place considered by Tibetan Buddhists to be the spiritual nucleus of a venerable network of sacred sites. Potala Palace was the chief residence of the fourteenth Dalai Lama until he was compelled to escape to India during the 1959 Tibetan uprising. When I visited, a group of heavily armed, grim-looking Communist Chinese military guards kept the local population under close scrutiny outside the palace. These menacing guards also intimidated our group of academic tourists, signalling us to move on and not to take their picture. My disdain and resentment for the invaders was in direct proportion to my admiration of the Tibetans.

Such mountain monasteries, and other ancient retreats of every description, continue to emanate a subtle magnetism, attracting pilgrims on life's obscure but very Grand Journey of Discovery. Due to the convenience of modern transportation, hundreds of millions of adherents visit pilgrimage sites worldwide every year, exponentially more than at any time in history. Some travel alone while others join all-inclusive trips. The religious tourist industry is big business. It even boasts its own academic publication—*The International Journal of Religious Tourism and Pilgrimage*—distributed by the Technological University in Dublin.

One of my first travel adventures was when my parents drove us across the border to Seattle where I saw the Space Needle, a Meccano-like tower that was erected for the Seattle World's Fair in 1962. This was only half a day's drive away from where I grew up, but I was tremendously impressed as a newly minted teen. My perception of what was possible was altered forever as I entered the realm of science fiction and rode on Seattle's elevated monorail, another "space age" wonder.

Drawn to great heights ever since, I have scaled the magical, mountain-like Borobudur Temple in Java, Indonesia (the largest Buddhist temple ever built) and been fortunate to have viewed skylines from atop the TV Tower in Berlin, the Oriental Pearl Tower in Shanghai, the Tokyo Tower in Japan and the CN Tower in Toronto. I have smoked a celebratory cigarillo with a friend from the pinnacle of the Eiffel Tower in Paris and scanned horizons from the heights of the Petronas Twin Towers in Kuala Lumpur, Malaysia (the globe's two tallest buildings from 1998 to 2004), as well as from the 110-storey Willis Tower and 100-storey John Hancock Center Observatory, both in Chicago.

In New York, I took a series of elevators to the top of the Empire State Building in 1963, when it was still the tallest building in the world (from 1931 to 1971), and visited the observation level and restaurant on the 106th and 107th floors of the former World Trade Center about twenty years before it was destroyed by two hijacked planes that were crashed into the buildings on September 11, 2001. Almost 3,000 people were killed and over 6,000 were injured, making it the deadliest terrorist attack in human history. Ground Zero has attained pilgrimage status with over six million visitors annually. I have also mounted the 162 stairs to the crown of the copper-clad Statue of Liberty from where I admired stunning views of the harbour, Brooklyn, lower Manhattan and Staten Island.

I have flown twice over Mount Everest, both times on clear days when it felt as if I could reach out and touch the fabled mountain in the Shangri-La of my mind, and have visited the lowest point on earth, distinguished by the mineral muds and floating atop the salt-encrusted waters of the Dead Sea. I reached both the North and South Poles, and I have descended to the depths of luminescent caves and explored steaming deserts, but my most remarkable and exhilarating travel experience was not at any of these locations. I have kept that escapade to myself for decades, unsure how I ought to describe it, if at all. It was a kind of two-part psychotic fugue, both embarrassing and nearly fatal, as I was simultaneously buried deeply in history and yet liberated by eternity. No, I am not talking about taking ayahuasca in the jungles of Peru...

NAKED IN A PYRAMID

My Self-Burial & Other Pursuits

IT WAS IN EGYPT, IN 1984, while I was visiting the 4,700-year-old Step Pyramid of Djoser at Saqqara, as well as the nearby necropolis of age-old Memphis, the seat of power for the pharaohs, that I came face-to-face with the enigmatic Sphinx and climbed the Great Pyramid of Giza, unsanctioned.

Erected in 2,560 BC at the edge of the Western Desert, approximately nine kilometres west of the Nile River, the Great Pyramid was the highest structure and most imposing stand-alone building for 4,000 years. It continues to be treasured today as the oldest of the Seven Wonders of the Ancient World and the only one remaining largely intact.

Earlier that fateful day, I, with a group, entered the once-hidden core of the largest of all pyramids, Cheops' House of Eternity, to access both the Queen's and the King's chambers. Hours later—with the help of *bakshish* and a long-shirted *gallibaya*-garbed guide named Ibrahim—I illegally began climbing the Great Pyramid at midnight.

I have never related a full account of this story since it happened to me forty years ago. After that fateful night on the mythically charged edifice, I sometimes feel I have been living on borrowed time, as if I am a ghost, a resurrected spirit, an ancient mariner condemned to tell his story so that I may warn others about their reckless inclinations.

According to the *Encyclopaedia Britannica*: "Although tourists were once able to freely climb the pyramids, that is now illegal. Offenders face up to three years in prison as penalty. In 2016 a teenage tourist was banned from visiting Egypt for life after posting photos and videos on social media of his illicit climb." The Egyptian government forbade climbing the pyramids in 1951 but the law was rarely enforced until 1973. Due to the steep inclines and awkward footing, the cumulative figures of deaths on the pyramids annually, multiplied by the 4,500 years, would easily amount to hundreds of thousands if one included all those who must have died during construction, those who mined the structures for building material, and those who climbed for adventure.

The height of the Great Pyramid is 449 feet, roughly equivalent to a 45-storey building if measured vertically, but the extended slant-height of each face is 610 feet. Having ascended from the desert floor at a precipitous 51.5° angle of incline and having already clambered over 200 feet into the forbidden Egyptian night, I was perched, like an insect, under the hypnotic gaze of a full moon, on the outer shell of the greatest building of antiquity.

I sat there on the immense stack of sculpted stones, about halfway up, wrestling with life and death. Suddenly petrified, I could neither continue the upward movement nor descend to *terra firma* below. Desperately searching for some way I might be rescued from the manufactured mountain, I imagined a helicopter dropping a rope and lifting me to safety.

Some may conjecture that I suffered a sudden attack of vertigo or acrophobia, but I believe it was more than that. Perhaps I am being overly dramatic in my efforts to assign meaning, but I also intuited that whatever "they say" about the pyramids being haunted was true. Even though I approached the grand mausoleum with reverence and meant no harm, the protective sentinels were impersonal furies, programed to defend their charges at all costs. It seemed that these age-old forces had conspired to repel me in any way they could. Some pushed, others pulled, while a third authority impregnated my lucid brain with a fierce fever of temporary insanity.

Gravity, the earth's jealous mistress, joined the assault and called out with an irresistible siren song begging me to succumb to her considerable charms. Seduced by a fatal attraction, the temptation to simply let go and tumble down the jagged pyramid was excruciatingly real; the desire to jump out from the side of the towering structure into the promised peace of annihilation was overbearing. Pharaoh Khufu's Guardian Spirit added its deadly presence to my torment, one that felt like I was being magnetically repulsed from the massive memorial.

In the midst of this mental maelstrom, suspended between heaven and earth, I felt like I was making love. A metaphysical orgasm was both the promised reward and the kiss of death. There was nothing between me and extinction as the psychotic madness inexorably overtook me. One more amorous thrust and my life would have ejaculated into oblivion. The French have a term for it—*la petite mort*.

At the same time, I knew that if I let myself be seduced by the Call of the Void, I would disappoint my teachers, those who organized the inspiring expedition to the heart of archaic Mediterranean cultures. Friends and family would be shocked, even devastated. I would also be sacrificing my future dreams and desires as the cherished gift of life would be squandered, defeated by a singular moment of delirium.

Somewhere in the back of my disappearing identity, I also remembered that the Torah directed us to "Choose life," and to "Guard yourself very well" for you have much to live for, much to accomplish for yourself and others. My falling into the desert night and being shattered against the huge limestone blocks would probably have been interpreted by others as a suicide or an accident whereas I meant it to be an expression of a flood of cosmic consciousness. The allure of sacred surrender to what felt like the complete love of the moment was so immediately powerful that it all seemed worthwhile.

This promise of letting go, opening my arms and falling into the all-encompassing embrace of the infinite, seemed like a moment of enlightenment and the fulfilment of my life's pilgrimage. If I died, however, I would not be there to explain my intentions to anyone or to celebrate my conjured piety.

I was one heartbeat, half a breath away from accepting what seemed like my glorious destiny and saying "yes" with every fibre of my body. Then, barely past the moment of no return, a surprising vision of future generations flooded my mind. I imagined surviving this ordeal and telling it to my children.

This was an illogical thought because I was not married and had no children at the time. If I succumbed to the Enchantress then I could not tell them the story in some theoretical future scenario. This desire or obligation to be a storyteller, to share my experience, was just enough to preserve my life.

Relieved yet still anxious, I turned back towards the millions of hulking blocks that served as a giant's stairway to Aaru—the idyllic Field of Reeds ruled by Osiris in Egyptian mythology—and, with my guide Ibrahim's assistance, I continued to scale my nemesis. Knowing I would never have such an opportunity again, I pushed myself through another frightening hour of slow climbing.

Since that night, I've often wondered why I didn't merely retreat from the colossal structure instead of daring to ascend to its peak another 250 dizzying feet towards the stars. I was still young and foolish enough— about thirty-five years old, the age of a veteran athlete—to want to accomplish this audacious feat. One hundred feet higher up, we came to what seemed like a cave. Upon closer inspection I surmised it was an area from which centuries of Egyptians, with the help of occasional earthquakes, had pushed some of the many-tonned blocks down the side of the pyramid to be used for buildings such as temples, homes, mosques and fortresses.

When I finally arrived at the top, I discovered that it had lost its cap and a few layers of stones making it about thirty feet shorter than when it was originally built 4,500 years ago. At one time, the entire pyramid was covered with a smooth cladding of highly polished white limestone and crowned with a large capstone that was rumoured to have been wrapped entirely in gold. The pharaoh's Mystic Mountain would have glowed with a spectral light day and night.

The flat area at the summit is about thirty feet in each direction and when I reached it, I was surprised to find two other explorers sleeping up there. I sat near the edge, surveying the thrilling 360° view of the vast moon-lit desert. Eventually, I was captivated by the other great nearby pyramid of Khafre, still clad at its top with the remnant of polished white stone, like snow anointing a mountain's peak. And there in the distance, facing due east in expectation of the rising sun, was the ever-enigmatic Sphinx.

A gentle ecstasy coursed through my body. I experienced a perfect moment of being present, of accomplishment and contentment. I was drunk with danger and exhausted with having grappled with mortality. It was, however, not yet time to fully relax.

I wanted to remain there forever but after about fifteen minutes it came time for us to descend. I was also concerned that I might be discovered and arrested by the police for trespassing on a heritage monument and endangering life—my own.

The descent took about an hour, my body carefully hugging each block before dropping onto the ledge of the one below. Meanwhile, the fellow I climbed with (he was also a member of our Mystery School but I hardly knew him nor did we communicate much during the experience), showed no signs of apprehension either in the ascent or descent. He reminded me of a young mountain goat skipping sure-footed among the rocks.

As we descended the Great Phenomenon, we eventually met up with four others who had started the midnight quest with us. Two of them were gripped with the same paralyzing fear as I had but at a lower elevation of about 100 feet. Two other nurturing friends remained with them for hours until we gathered ourselves and our wits together and gradually completed our return to the safety of the desert plateau.

As I slipped off the last megastone, I dropped to the ground and kissed it with deep gratitude at having survived. It was about 5 a.m. but still dark. We walked to the all-night café at Mena House, the classic British-era pink sand-coloured hotel dating from the late nineteenth century, where we were staying. We ordered an early breakfast—I treated myself to a double order of hash browns and a large mug of hot chocolate—and, between yawns of well-earned exhaustion, recounted our stories.

I was deeply humbled to be alive, resurrected really, and joyous to have succeeded in such a memorable feat. Hubris, however, was never part of the equation: I tremble whenever I recollect this forbidden venture, the angst returns and my respect for the preciousness of life is renewed.

I have since revealed this drama to my adult children—and now you, Dear Reader—so the story cycle is complete and the vision fulfilled. But there was to be an unexpected Act Two to the Great Adventure, also one that I would never dare engage in again. The allure of Egypt gave rise to an equally soul-stirring, more private exploit, one that took all my equanimity, perspective and physical strength to complete…

Early the next afternoon, I began the long climb down to the subterranean chambers beneath the Great Pyramid, an area inaccessible to the general public. It was not from the side of the great structure but rather from a ground-level, locked gate away from all the others. Our small group from the Jean Houston Mystery School had obtained official permission from the Egyptian Ministry of State for Antiquities to access the caverns via this marginal entrance, secured by an iron door fitted with a heavy lock. [After fifty years of exploring, Dr. Jean Houston continues to develop Mystery School programs that meld ancient teachings from a variety of cultures with her own stimulating insights and the latest discoveries in neuroscience, philosophy, spirituality and psychology.] With an "Open Sesame," the chains fell away.

We descended cautiously, backwards, down a low, narrow, dim, claustrophobia-inducing shaft that led to two large subterranean chambers a hundred feet beneath the pyramid. Only a few of us carried flashlights to illuminate the diagonal passageway for the others. I used both my hands for the arduous semi-dark descent into the netherworld. The chiselled rock passageway was not tall enough to stand up in, so we had to remain crouched over. Most of the time we lowered ourselves slowly on our hands and knees or upon our bellies.

There was only enough room for one person to navigate at a time, either descending or ascending, and, as happened, if one of us was suddenly struck with a claustrophobic panic attack and needed to escape to the surface, they had to wait for the others to pause in what were somewhat larger crevices where two people could pass, albeit with some difficulty.

The air was dank and stale. Sound was muted, dense, almost non-existent. We navigated more by touch and trust than by sight or logic. Some of us became mortified that the mammoth complex composed of 2,300,000 blocks of stone weighing some 6,500,000 tons, and condensed over 13 acres of land, might collapse upon us. We felt that we were about to suffer a horrific demise but were quickly reassured by our guide that the pyramid had stood for 4,500 years; it was not about to abruptly destruct now.

Nonetheless, the deeper we descended, the thinner the oxygen became and we were in danger of hallucinating if we remained underground too long. Anxiety gripped us every dark step of the way and yet I felt I was willing to sacrifice everything—to die to my limited self, to become a martyr in my search for the elusive "beloved." At that point, however, she was wearing her ominous, suffocating death mask, not the face of radiant beauty and reassuring wonder. This was no fantasy nor was it a dream from which I might awaken. I share these sensations with you reluctantly even now, wary of reigniting the trauma.

After about twenty minutes of inching down the narrow passageway, we arrived at what seemed like two large caverns with high ceilings and a series of sub-caves. The purpose of these subterranean chambers excavated by the early Egyptians remains a mystery. It is possible that they were originally intended to be the pharaoh's final resting place but that was changed to the King's Chamber concealed higher up within the structure. Mostly shrouded in shadows cast by our guide's lantern, I saw just enough to regain my bearings.

Letting the others proceed, I chose a secluded corner of one of the rough-hewn caverns and there—in the dark, bereft of cover, and interred in the majestic sepulchre—I removed my clothes. Having abandoned the trappings of civilization and perceiving nothing but an ethereal cradle of Pure Essence, I emptied my mind and contemplated existence.

In the belly of the beast, I performed one more unthinkable act. No, not that. Although I imagine that, over the centuries, more than one expression of frenzied passion had been consummated in the chasmic womb of Egypt.

In my small backpack, I had a bottle of water and my *tefillin* (phylacteries), modest leather boxes, with dangling leather straps, containing Hebrew texts—Jewish prayer amulets inscribed with words from the Torah. I placed one of them around my head, something that helped to activate my crown chakra. The second one was wrapped seven times around my left arm and hand as a sign of aligning physical action with spiritual forces.

It might have been the only time in history this was done in a pyramid—certainly by a man as naked as Adam. It connected me to the heritage of my birth tradition as a member of the biblical tribe of Levi, and to the Exodus from the very civilization that built this extraordinary structure. I also felt a direct link to Abraham and Sarah who emerged from Mesopotamia 4,800 years previously. I allowed my psyche to wander into the heart of heaven, there to engage the Infinite, the All and the No Thing.

Knowing that I might be underground for a relatively short time, appreciating that this was an extremely rare experience, and cloaked in an atmosphere of palpable fear, I focused meditative imagery, using the formidable power of the pyramid directly overhead to amplify its effects. Opinions, beliefs and directions melted away; history was both fulfilled and erased; the personal gave way to the universal; I was simultaneously vibrant like never before and extinguished as never again.

An hour later, upon emerging from the earth into fresh air and warm sunlight, fully clothed and overflowing with gratitude, I felt reborn, wrung from the birth canal all over again.

Photograph of Marilyn Monroe (Norma Jeane Baker) by Milton H. Greene, 1954. Y.W. commissioned this unique crop of the image.

MOTEL EARTH

SHE HAD A SHORT, CONVOLUTED, fabulous, torturous, successful, manipulated life. Adored by millions, she was lonely. She became a symbol, a mythic archetype, and bore the burden of our projections.

It killed her. We killed her.

It was one of those situations that I even remember when it happened and where I was. It was just over four months into my thirteenth year; we were in Penticton, staying at the Crown Motel on Lake Okanagan for summer vacation. August 4, 1962.

The news was on the b&w television and printed in oversize headlines in a special, salmon-pink-paper edition of the *Vancouver Sun*. This was my first conscious experience of someone committing suicide because of life trauma. I didn't, couldn't, fully understand it at the time, but never forgot the shock.

Years later, after the untimely deaths of Jim Morrison, Brian Jones, Janis Joplin, Jimi Hendrix, Kurt Cobain and Amy Winehouse, each at twenty-seven years of age, and others such as Elvis, who died in 1977, I saw a pattern and thought about the pressures of success.

When Michael Jackson died on Thursday, June 25, 2009—also the result of psychological pressures and botched drugs—I started thinking even more seriously about retiring from Simon Fraser University and moving on with my life.

I realized that it was "we," the public, who killed him, as well as Marilyn and all the rest. They bought into fame, something that often comes with a death sentence. We—the fans who could not do what they could so we projected our ideals upon them—absorbed what they fed us and depleted them.

It is not that any one particular person pulled the trigger. It was rather a symptom of the human mind, a psyche that has evolved in the image of universal consciousness and that lives beneath the mask of metaphor, fooled by the illusion that it is real.

We are a tribe of performers and voyeurs. Some of us dance, sing, act, write, run, govern, manage, joke, inspire; several are on stage at the urban Orpheum and in legendary Eleusinian fields.

The rest of us sit in the audience, paying the price of admission, watching Mr. Bojangles dance himself to death to feed our unfulfilled needs as we goad him on with razor-lined applause before exiting the side door into a dark and ominous lane.

About ten years ago, I realized that I, too, had become numb to myself. I was acting as others might expect me to perform, a community thespian in their play, becoming a tragedy with only scattered laughs to set the scene and eventual downfall. My name had become a commodity, my thoughts were someone else's, my words read from a long-rehearsed script.

Within a few months, I made some major decisions in business and life priorities. I gave notice at SFU (but in a responsible manner to maintain the principal programs), purchased a cottage on Bowen Island, removed myself from contentious business dealings with my siblings, dropped off of most boards and committees, cut back on donations, and embarked on dream-fulfilling travels to Tibet, Bhutan, Cambodia, Indonesia, China, Japan, Singapore, etc.

And I began writing more. I allowed myself to die a non-mortal death so that I would not yet have to check out of Motel Earth.

I renewed my resolve a few years later when I turned seventy and circumnavigated the planet, fully aware of the physical correspondences between geography and body, as well as the emotional, spiritual and intellectual relationships between the global brain and the extended human mind. These itinerant travels helped to literally *ground* me. I have since been renouncing more communal and self-imposed burdens, further settling business affairs. I am dedicating these remaining years to mining the hidden words concealed so well within, and further divesting myself from the cannibalistic needs of society.

After that ego death, there was a resurrection into a still unfolding world and series of opportunities.

From Marilyn's tortured overdose in '62 until today, over six decades have transpired. She, too, has proven to be one of my teachers.

From being a model who aroused teenage desire, to becoming a life lesson for the price of fame, she ultimately serves as a tender touchstone for empathy.

In the summer of 2011, on his way to the North Pole, Yosef Wosk visited Moscow and St. Petersburg and discovered that, though they were very different cities, they were both home to magnificent treasures and memorials. Among his pilgrimages was a visit to the graves of Russian cultural luminaries including Pyotr Ilyich Tchaikovsky (1840–1893) and Fyodor Mikhailovich Dostoevsky (1821–1881), both of whom are buried in the Necropolis of the Masters of Art adjacent to the imposing Aleksander Nevsky Monastery.– Ed.

DOSTOEVSKY'S GHOST

RUSSIAN ORTHODOX NUNS—modestly garbed head-to-foot in flowing black robes, on their way to pray at the Nevsky Monastery—mixed with other worshippers and a menagerie of tourists, as our guide led us through an ornate iron gate to enter the cultural pantheon in the Land of the Living Dead.

After some historical orientation, I left our private tour behind and surreptitiously returned to Dostoevsky's sculptural tomb. Once there, I cast a furtive glance in every direction to reassure myself that we were alone—Fyodor and Yosef, a prodigal son.

I felt a certain camaraderie with the Russian authors. My father was born in Odessa in 1917 in the shadow of the Bolshevik Revolution and a constant stream of murderous pogroms. I was also distantly related to Dostoevsky through geography: In the sixteenth century his ancestral family had been granted land near Pińsk (then part of the Grand Duchy of Lithuania, later part of Poland and today in Belarus). His family name was derived from a nearby village, Dostoievo, old Polish for dignitary. My mother's family also hailed from Pińsk, where she was born in 1917. She once confided to me that we were related to the family of Isaac Bashevis Singer, who was later awarded a Nobel Prize for literature. She remembered a visit from the Singer [Zynger] family when she was still a child in Pińsk. My mother and her two sisters, however, were warned to never disclose that they were also related to Leon Trotsky, born Lev Davidovich Bronstein. They had been told to keep it a strict secret out of fear that Stalin's henchmen might also threaten Trotsky's relatives, among them our family. Eventually, Trotsky would be hunted down and assassinated in Mexico City in 1940.

Standing now before Dostoevsky's grave, I caught my breath and gathered my thoughts. For the next few minutes I lost myself in a contemplative conversation with the great writer who had endured fame and criticism to become a celebrated figure beyond the borders of his birth; a man who had served as an inspired conduit for the written word and suffered for the sake of the ideal. At Dostoevsky's funeral, 100,000 mourners had accompanied his coffin through the streets of St. Petersburg to this very spot. It didn't matter that he had been deceased for 130 years.

Standing before the bronze and granite reliquary, I, the Idiot, asked the Holy Fool:

"What is my path forward? Will I be a writer at last? Should I abandon everything else and finally accept this calling? I'm getting older, my strength is waning. What must I do?"

In a dialogue of souls, he was the buried one but I considered him to be more alive than I had ever dared to be. I was the Underground Man, the furtive seeker, frightened of authentic freedom, fearful to escape my domesticated, tamed, trained, graded and judged self. My query was not just about writing. It was a metaphor for existence. Shaded by the maple tree standing guard before his lifelike bust, I looked into Fyodor's piercing eyes and implored in the silence for his guidance:

"What if I am not a good enough writer? What if my words are mocked? Rejected? Worse, what if I am dismissed as a bore? In a world already saturated with other people's finely-attired opinions, what if I have nothing profound to say? Or my rhymes were out of tune?"

Channeling both hope and humility, my soul-to-soul encounter with the Ghost of Dostoevsky Past seemed somehow illicit but entirely necessary. I had transformed the astute novelist into a Siberian shaman, imploring his intercession with the God of Arts & Letters, hoping he might perform an act of improbable magic on my behalf. In a heightened state of ecstasy and fear, I wanted him to have the supernatural power to lift up my hand, raise the quill and dip its shaved nib into a cracked bottle of blood-red ink. But perhaps there was nothing noble about my quest? Perhaps my pilgrimage was to be pitied?

There I was, a delusional man of sixty-two, deliberating with the remnants of a great talent's spectre who died from a cacophony of ailments when he, himself, was only fifty-nine years old. When alive, Dostoevsky had used his days to gather words in a bountiful harvest whereas even if I had stumbled across a flowered phrase or inspired idea I often let it wilt, foolishly promising myself that I would remember it, that I would return when ready, when I was in the mood to arrange each flowered word as a bouquet of perfect prose.

Now our roles were reversed. I was reminded of the mocking motto in a Latin cemetery: *Quod tu es, ego fui. Quod ego sum, tu eris.* "What you are, I once was. What I am now, you soon will be." I, the Underground Man, called from the crypt of my own discontent. Eventually, the haunting voice of the weary ghost of Dostoevsky reverberated through the church yard:

"You are drowning in illusion, enchanted by reverie, addicted to the future. You must dispel the fantasy, wake from the dream, shatter the mirror of your own reflection and, with the shards, sever the bonds that restrain you.

"You cannot be a writer without picking up the pen, defiling the paper, working and then diligently mining one draft after another. You must dedicate daily hours to this necessary labour even if it kills you as it did me.

"Only after sacrificing your life can you be resurrected into an expanded sense of self. Or better yet, forget yourself. Unless you die to your limitations, abandoning all that conspires to defeat you, you will merely exist but never truly live.

"Perhaps, Yosef, or whatever your real name is, you are *not* a writer. There are many ways to be creative. Sing if you want; weave if you must; build, dance, love, destroy, be kind. Become a thief, an artist, a craftsman, architect or a friend. Your *crime* may be that you have mistakenly chosen the wrong vehicle; your *punishment* is that it has absorbed your years, robbed what little time you have and squandered your particular gift.

"There is no meaning, no purpose, no grand scheme. There are billions of you, the inconsequential product of endless blind desire. You are no more or less important than dappled dust suspended in the morning sun.

"You are a prisoner of your own restless mind, infected with confusion and mirage, catapulted from one corner of the cosmos to the other. You have already written much but not enough. Put your affairs in order; take care of those who depend upon you but do not be overly burdened by their incessant needs. Drop your distracting activities and enter deep into the Kingdom of Words. Your writing will be a strict yet nourishing taskmaster: demanding, decisive, and precious.

"Write like you are a beggar hungry for any scrap but starving for the precise word. You must have the stamina of an athlete, sharpness of an executioner, ruthlessness of a soldier, freedom of the wind and passion of a lover.

"All that came before will inform you but be very jealous of your time for it evaporates, imperceptibly, never to return."

As his voice faded with the afternoon light and the ghost was recalled to its nocturnal grave, I heard the faint echo of his concluding words:

"I bless and encourage you to only be your original self. You are on the right path. After all, you were led here to my distant grave. The time has come. *Zhivi poka zhiv.* Live while you are alive. *Proshchaniye.* Farewell."

The Legend had no reason to lie, to flatter, to deceive or cajole. In the end he was reassuring, telling me that all I had experienced in life, the hundreds of paths I had followed, all led to this point. Those experiences were to be integrated; none ignored. I felt a curious calmness settle over me.

Not a word was spoken but much had been said. I did not turn away but bowed my head and retreated three steps, as one does when in the presence of majesty.

A brief nod to Tchaikovsky, then I left the cemetery.

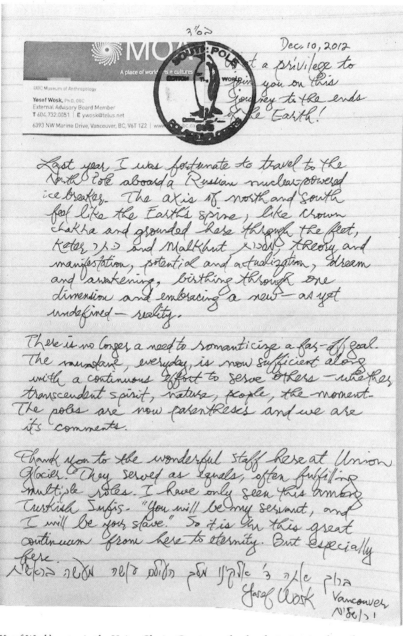

בס״ד

Dec. 10, 2012

... t a privilege to ... you on this ... journey to the ends ... e Earth!

Last year I was fortunate to travel to the North Pole aboard a Russian nuclear-powered ice breaker. The axis of north and south feel like the Earth's spine; like crown chakra and grounded here through the feet, Keter כתר and Malkhut מלכות, theory and manifestation, potential and actualization, dream and awakening, birthing through one dimension and embracing a new — as yet undefined — reality.

There is no longer a need to romanticize a far-off goal. The mundane, everyday, is now sufficient along with a continuous effort to serve others — whether transcendent spirit, nature, people, the moment. The poles are now parentheses and we are its comments.

Thank you to the wonderful staff here at Union Glacier. They served as equals, often fulfilling multiple roles. I have only seen this among Turkish Sufis: "You will be my servant, and I will be your slave." So it is in this great continuum from here to eternity. But especially here.

ברוך אתה ה' אלהינו מלך העולם שהכל נהיה בדברו

Yosef Wosk
Vancouver
יוסף וסק

Yosef Wosk's entry in the Union Glacier Camp guestbook, after returning from the South Pole approximately 600 nautical miles (1,111 km) away and providing the place name for Mt. Serrat.

UBC Museum of Anthropology

Yosef Wosk, Ph.D., OBC
External Advisory Board Member
T 604.732.0051 | E ywosk@telus.net
6393 NW Marine Drive, Vancouver, BC, V6T 1Z2 | www...

SOUTH POLE

I.

On this planeload of all ages
with 27 languages among us,
there is but one way:
south, south, forever south,
to one of only two points on earth
where all directions disappear.

The only portal of escape
is to turn oneself inside out
and discover the lone path of return
to the Northern Kingdom.
We have sacrificed everything
to arrive at our destination
where the entire world balances on a pin.
We follow a relentless compass path,
drawn by imagination's gravity,
south, south, forever south,
beyond civilizations infected
with their human theatrics

that gradually contaminated a once pristine planet.
It is the final terrestrial frontier,
where—frightened by what we have wrought—
we have limited our activity
to protect ourselves from ourselves
and our planet from being further cultivated,
settled, monetized and raped.
Perhaps salvation exists
where humans have the least impact,
in the *Terra Australis Incognito,*
where we will soon waddle
among tuxedo-garbed penguins.

II.

Guarding the Western Hemisphere's approach to the Antarctic,
at the tip of South America,
we wing our way over nameless Chilean villages.
I wonder who lives beneath us? for how long?
Will their grandchildren tell traditional stories?
Call the past sacred for another ten thousand years?
Or will they abandon these mountains and valleys,
seduced by tales of urban splendour?
Who can blame them either way?
How did they get there? Will they fight to stay?
Do they ever glance up at these sleek silver air ships
and sense we're speeding to some elsewhere
across the distant southern horizon?

The Chileans seem a beautiful, friendly race.
They have tightly pulled-back black hair and dark eyes.
On the plane, as crews change, they take care

to greet one another with a kiss that is
most often accompanied by a smile.
Not the double European style but rather
a single brushing of cheeks and a side kiss.
Their Spanish is gentle, lyrical.
Our English seems brusque, harsh.
Most of us are from other countries.
I try to identify any locals, any pure-bred *Indios*
whose ancestors could have arrived on these shores
on Polynesian rafts so many millennia ago.
Or do most people hereabouts
still accept that North American theory
about the land bridge from Aleutian Asia?
I don't stare, knowing I'm an invader
disguised as a guest.
Amid the scientists and tourists
our foreign tongues pervade
but there are many *mestizos*,
mixtures of Spanish and Indigenous descent,
half of this and half of that,
some of this with a portion of that,
drawn together by irresistible attractions,
beauty in the service of sex;
abandoning loneliness
and gratefully surrendering
to the biological imperative
so that a species might survive.

III.

It is the fullness of spring,
just nineteen days shy of winter's solstice.

It's five o'clock and darkness
has not yet cast its determined shadow.
Herein lies the confusion,
for much earlier this double day I crossed the equator:
What once was winter in the north
was transformed into a southern summer,
and autumn renamed spring.
Having flown through the Looking Glass
I wonder if I am still the same person as before
or one in bewildering reverse?
Not that it matters,
for I have embarked on this expedition to
the ends of the earth to escape memory and rules,
to transcend limitations and liberate logic,
to enter the Great Beyond
where poetry reigns and story rules.

Sitting by the window at 10,000 feet
I feel the warmth of my waffle-knit,
burgundy sweater upon my right shoulder.
What an enchanting gift of sunshine.
I am travelling south on an Airbus,
three-and-a-half hours from Santiago,
but the sun has radiated this warmth
from a hundred million miles away
to light my pen,
to toast my shoulder,
to nurture my hibernating senses.
In this moment of unexpected levity,
gratitude flows through me like blood.
Finally, after a lifetime of dreaming
and a year of planning,

I am nearing the southern-most tip
of the twin American land mass.
We are approaching the Land of Fire,
still on the maps as *Tierra del Fuego*,
bound for Cape Horn and the Strait of Magellan
at the great convergence of three Sister Seas
named by cartographers
who like to fill in the blanks,
to bestow labels, honour explorers and their patrons,
to christen the world as it emerges
from the fog of unknowing.
It is here that the briny, deep triplets
merge in stormy seas,
each contributing its weathered personality:
the warm Pacific from the west,
turbulent Atlantic currents from the east,
colliding with cold, southern, Antarctic waters.
They are local ambassadors, often at war,
a circus of circulation,
the leading edges of the One World Ocean
that covers most of the planet's surface
with her iridescent liquid cloak.

I am startled back to the present
as we drop through the clouds
for two days of orientation in Punta Arenas.
There will be thirteen of us going further
to the Hidden Continent,
a new neverland
so distant, cold and formidable
that even the ubiquitous *Homo sapiens*
avoided any settlement

until our own generations followed in the footsteps of
the Heroic Age of Antarctic Exploration,
of the stern-faced Amundsen (December 14, 1911)
and tragically doomed Scott (January 17, 1912).
Having come this far,
having given up everything,
we further surrender ourselves
to the mythic imperative.

In a few days, at last, we will tumble
over the edge of the earth,
out of our minds,
to inhabit the archetypes of extreme
geographic and psychological travel.
We will discard our well-cultivated identities
in favour of citizenship in a metaverse
where imagination transcends thought.
All the rest is unknown
in the land of the yet-to-be.
Possibly words, too, will end.
I am prepared to be welcomed
by a new silence.

IV.

In Punta Arenas, logistics kick in.
I don't recognize Sergei and Dimitri,
two Russians from my trip to the North Pole,
but they remember me.
As if to justify his memory and tales of acclaimed travel,
Sergei searches through ten thousand photographs
like a magician shuffling his deck of trick cards.

There, still trapped within the mechanical mind
of his most trusted camera,
was a petrified picture of me
at the other edge of the earth.
Déjà vu all over again.
Perhaps it was our shared bi-polarity
that we had in common.
Having stood at one geographic extreme,
there was only one way left to go.
One begins to crave completion
in the back streets of the global 'hood.

There's an early wake-up for all.
The equipment check is at 9 a.m.
Boots bought in Vancouver pass muster.
I used 'em on Baffin Island.
To make sure clothing is warm enough
to protect against the cold and killing winds,
Olivia—thousands of miles from her home in Terrace, B.C.—
checks what I brought for the remote expedition.
Cold weather travel discourages cotton;
instead wool and engineered synthetics
are recommended to whisk away sweat
and keep the body fresh and warm.
I've complied and passed yet another hurdle
on the obstacle course of survival.

Orientation is at 10:30.
We feel like astronauts,
our bodies entombed in exoskeletons of polar protection.
I'm handed a hard-to-miss red parka
and pants of insulating fleece.

A borrowed balaclava from the company store
cradles my head and becomes a best friend forever.

With time to spare, I walk the town,
taking photos of weathered buildings
embellished with witty Spanish graffiti.
They seem like a counter-cultural confessional.
Pizza for lunch, universal
(it is warm, familiar and flavourful:
comfort food where everything else is strange).
To the east, the Argentinian town of Ushaia
also claims the tourist title of
southernmost city in the world.
It, too, has hotels and restaurants
named *Fin del Mundo*.
Sitting in the pub gazing at the casual
assembly of boats in the harbour,
I suddenly realize these frigid waters
are an extension of the same ones
that wash the shores
of my far-off home in Vancouver.
But I can't travel north to get there.
I can't do anything now except go south,
lemming-like, south, south, only south.
It is disconcerting, and yet exhilarating,
to conclude that the only way home
must be in the opposite direction.
This was my Last Long Walk
before turning my back on the Americas.

My bag, carefully crowded with irreplaceable items,
goes to the airport ahead of me.

We all have stay-behind luggage
for non-essential possessions.
I will take just one book
but spend my time reading the landscape.
I am ready on the morning of December 5th
for our initial 1,000-mile flight to Union Glacier
on an impressive, veteran
Russian Ilyushin-76TD transport plane
as if I'm part of some tourist military.
We will camp for a week on the glacier—
that massive river of frozen antipodal ice—
while awaiting clear weather for the fight to the Pole.
If, during that parenthesis of six days
conditions don't provide safe passage,
we will have travelled the earth
but not achieved our purpose.

Antarctica is the coldest, driest, windiest
and most remote place on earth.
It has the highest average elevation of all the continents
and is also the largest desert in the world,
a desert defined not by temperature
but by a rainfall of ten inches or less per year.
My head spins in wonder
as we prepare to concede the spoils of civilization
for inconvenience and consider it an adventure;
a return to raw uncooked nature,
to a place that Scott referred to as

> *Great God! This is an awful place and terrible enough for us to have laboured to it without the reward of priority. Well, it is something to have got here, and the wind may be our friend tomorrow. Now for the*

run home and a desperate struggle. I wonder if we can do it.

No showers for a week and
washing only with melted ice
in a small bowl—that would be easy.
Leaving myself behind,
that was the deeper destination,
the more difficult goal.
This trip was not a mere physical journey.
Reaching a geographic extreme was
a necessary step in
shamanic psychogeography.
We spend years trying to be noticed
as an indication that we are alive,
have significance, and will survive,
but what happens if we deconstruct
our personalities and plan to disappear,
not be a nuisance, not be noticed at all?
I felt I was willing to sacrifice myself—
not on an altar of fire but one of ice.
Whatever it took: *Hineini.* "Here I am."
My life of lost and found
could lead to one invisible door
that I alone recognized.
A veritable Sabbath dwelled within.
Not just a seventh day or
a seventh continent.
A seventh kabbalistic soul.

These were among my final contemplations
as we were bundled aboard
and winged our way

south, south, forever south,
swallowed by an ancient aircraft,
a classically beautiful workhorse
with a big belly and transparent bubble nose.
The plane had been usurped by its crew
in Kazakhstan in 1987,
as the Soviet Union was crumbling,
essentially stolen by profiteers and mercenaries,
flying contraband, soldiers, medical aid or us.
Have plane for hire; no questions asked,
No reasonable offer refused.

The crew is still Russian.
This was and remains a cargo plane.
A semblance of seats were added
for only about one-third of the space.
The original interior remains cavernous,
18-feet high and curved on the sides
and yet it is claustrophobic
because there are so few windows.
On the twin frontiers of reverie and reality
I sink back into slumber, reminding myself,
"It is this for which I asked. Dream on."

V.

Over two continents
and now towards a third.

VI.

It takes us four hours to reach Union Glacier,
another place I'd never seen in an atlas.

This is not just in the middle of nowhere.
It feels more like it *is* nowhere.

When at last we skid along the rare blue-ice runway
I utter a silent prayer of thanksgiving,
acknowledging that everything in my life has led
to this memorable moment of birth.
We get off the plane to a sparkling wonderland
of bright ice and 25 km/hour breeze.
I turn to take one-handed, gloved photos
of our now handsome and muscular plane.
Unscripted, I think back to the first landing on the moon
when Neil Armstrong—unable to see his own breath
between draughts of bottled oxygen—
was told exactly what to say.
I don't envy him.

We walk to a hut for instructions.
There is no immigration.
There is no country.
Some have claimed parts of the continent
but, in an effort to assuage human greed,
the Antarctic Treaty was eventually signed to
dedicate it to peace and science,
a continent uniquely shared by all.
For now.

We are driven twelve-at-a-time
in a jeep-like SUV vehicle,
with tires exchanged for tank treads,
to Union Glacier Camp
where we are given orientation:

Beware of light planes landing.
Beware of crevices opening up
that swallow you as in *Star Wars.*
Here's how to use the toilets.
Here's the communal dining tent.
Here are the two-person sleeping tents
called clams due to their shape.
My tent-mate is Rajesh
from India. A good match.
Both former Brit colonials.
We share sensibilities.
We are both vegetarians.

There are three orientation sessions.
Rajesh and I take notes. No one else bothers.
The South Pole in the Antarctic
is land surrounded by water,
whereas the North Pole in the Arctic
is water surrounded by land.
We also learn that
there are seven south poles.

1. *Ceremonial South Pole* is set up outside the American research station a few hundred yards from the South Geographic Pole. Since the station drifts every year on its icesheet, a decorated Ceremonial Pole—surrounded by flags of the original twelve signatories to the Antarctic Protocol—was established for visitors and official ceremonies.

2. *Geographic South Pole* is where all the lines of longitude converge, the point where the earth rotates on its axis. Geographic South Pole is a fixed geographic location, 90° S. It never moves even if, over billions of years, oceans and continents drift beneath its gaze.

3. *South Magnetic Pole* is moveable. For two hundred years, it has shifted at an average of about 9 km. to the northwest. It is now found in the Southern Ocean about 2,850 kilometres from the South Geographic Pole.

4. *South Pole of Inaccessibility* is the centre of Antarctica, the point furthest from the sea (whereas in the Arctic it's the point equidistant from surrounding land masses).

5. *South Pole of Cold* is the coldest point of the coldest place on earth.

6. There is also a *South Pole of Rotation*.

7. And a *South Celestial Pole*.

There are just as many corresponding poles to the North. The Equator is halfway between the Geographic Poles, precisely 10,000 kilometres from each.

Antarctic means "opposite to the arctic." Arctic is derived from the Greek *arktos* ("bear"). Not for white polar bears, but for the northern constellation of the Bear overhead.

We are now all on New Zealand time.
Safety, safety, safety.
At last there is an apple, remnant
of the carefully stocked food tent,
exotic, like a revival drug,
in my Antarctic-rated sleeping bag.
It reminds me how far we have wandered
from the Garden of Eden,
from any garden, grass or flower
here in the Frosted Forest of No Trees
except beneath the cold Southern Sea
that flourishes with astounding abundance.

After all the planning, fantasizing, and doubts,

I am present now to a new reality.
The only sounds are those that inhabit my private world:
the ebb and flow of tidal breath,
beating of my open heart,
and the slowing parade of my monkey-mind
that reclines into a more peaceful tranquility
as the incessant stimulations of civilization's roar
recedes into an ever-distant past.

It is so silent here
that it hurts my ears.
It takes me three days to more fully adjust.
For a moment I reflect upon my ancestors,
upon all existence leading to this moment.
My parents escaped from horrors
to afford me this freedom.
Perhaps I took their emigration
to a more radical conclusion,
continuing their exodus to the very ends of the earth.
"Away from here, away from here.
Nothing else will ever do.
South, south and ever south."

I feel grateful for the labours of past generations
and, without diminishing my own efforts,
I also feel responsible
for the fulfillment of their violated visions;
to accommodate them and to cultivate
the pregnancy of their aborted dreams.
In the stillness of an eyeless ice,
I birth the world back into itself
as it was once meant to ever be.

VII.

The long-anticipated flight to the pole
is 600 miles and four hours away.
The aircraft is a 1940s heritage DC-3,
still sleek as a sports car and strong as a mule.
Flying on this beloved low-wing metal monoplane
was one of the highlights of the trip.
I took so many photographs of the twin propellered
Art Nouveau silver craft
that it became a kind of consolation:
Even if we couldn't reach the object of our desire
I would have at least flown
in one of the world's most beautiful machines.

Two or three days after landing on Union Glacier,
(I'd lost track of time
due to the 24-hour summer sun)
there are ideal conditions at both ends.
We hasten our loading procedures.
Take-off in one hour is announced
for the final flight to the Pole.
Eleven of the passengers are Russian,
one Indian and me, the lone Canadian.
A guide accompanies us as does a medical officer.
The pilots were also Canadian because the aircraft
was rented from Kenn Borek out of Edmonton,
a company that specializes in
extreme flights throughout the world.
It is December 6, 2012,
just over a century since Amundsen and then Scott
first arrived at the most desolate spot on earth.

A year after our excursion,
international news headlines
announce the tragic crash of a Twin Otter
operated by the same company.
The fatal flight, in which three men died
and whose bodies remain entombed
on one of the Frozen Continent's highest mountains,
was on its way from the South Pole with a load of fuel
for an Italian research team at Terra Nova Bay.
It is a sobering reminder that
this is no regular undertaking:
There are risks wrapped in peril.
I am aloft within a dream,
hopefully not a nightmare.

At last, we reach the (geographic) South Pole!
We land on wheels retrofitted with skis.
It is too cold to kneel and kiss the ground
(even in the December summer sun
it is -30° C outside)
but I greet it with a warm smile
and a certain sense of accomplishment.
Time and space are abstract here,
more a concept than tangible reality.
All of the earth's 24 time zones meet at this point:
It can be any time—
any hour, any minute, any second—
or no time at all.
Similarly, here, as in its Northern counterpart,
all space converges on the polar point.
In one short jaunt around a ceremonial mast
decorated as a red, white and blue striped barber's pole

crowned with a golden orb,
I pass through all time zones and
complete a walkabout of the planet.
No jet lag for having travelled twenty-four hours
in a matter of seconds
and no exhaustion for having encircled the planet
in twelve short steps.
Only elation.
Today I embrace the planet,
the original cathedral,
and bask in a geographic joy of consuming pleasure
here beyond the road less travelled
in the Realm of Timeless Starlight.

A guide from the American-run
Amundsen-Scott South Pole Station
takes us for an extended tour of the impressive facilities.
The buildings—constructed on hydraulic lifts
to keep above the accumulating snows—
drift about 30 feet each year with the ice sheet.
Entering the library I am surprised
to see an upside-down globe.
The south is at the top.
I absent-mindedly approach
to correct it, to turn it around.
Then it struck me:
"Why shouldn't south be on top?"
It was an iconoclastic moment.
I abruptly realized how we were enslaved
to the dictates of a northern monopoly.
Our assigning North as the upper dimension

is merely the result of a narrow cultural conceit.

Before leaving the station
we visit the small souvenir shop.
I find a treasured lapel pin emblazoned
with the initials OAE—*Old Antarctic Explorer.*
From now on, every direction will only head north.
There is absolutely nowhere else to turn.

VIII.

We arrive back at Union Glacier
not long after a midnight that is still so bright
that many wear sunglasses.
An hours-long banquet has been prepared for us,
irrigated with wine, beer, champagne
and vodka after lucent vodka that I drink
with my new-found Russian friends.
The more we drink, the better brothers we become,
at least for that now-sacred night of the celebrating soul.

Four hours to the pole;
Four hours at our destination;
Fours hours to return to base camp.
We did not have to trek through blinding blizzards
or eat our sledge dogs to survive,
but it did take a lifetime of audacious ambition
and years of careful planning to finally arrive here.
We realize that we are among the fortunate few
who will ever visit the true Land's End.
I am thankful and exceedingly relieved
at having passed this self-imposed examination

marking the limits of my mettle.
Who could ask for anything more?
I go to sleep at 3 a.m.
I wake at 6 a.m. to Rajesh shaving.
I try to sleep but am not tired.

The weather window is open to flying
for only one more day and a plane to Punta Arenas
will leave in a few hours.
Expedition travel is contingent upon tens of intangibles
but especially the weather.
If we don't leave now
we will have to stay for another week
until another plane can be procured
and the weather is clear again.
As for me, it feels absurd to desert
this hard-won icebound acreage
since I know I will never be here again.
Every moment is a precious gift;
every step is as a toddler's first on a cryogenic planet
millions of light years from our own.
Although the Pole was my ultimate goal
I also welcome the vast wilderness
and profound solitudes of the Antarctic dreamscape.
I have come here not for human culture—
artificial creations, stimulating attractions
and wasteful distractions—
but to escape their ubiquitous, invasive presence.
For what *isn't* here.
Far from the madding noise,
the stress and commanding list of appointments.
Far from those who want this and expect that;

sheltered from those who demand,
from those who drain the spirit from me.
In this pristine air, I need only accept
the feat of being one of a scattered thousand
on an entire continent.

To help them decide whether to remain,
some gather around maps with the expedition leader
to see if they'll be enticed
by what to do, where to go, what to learn,
for the next few days.
Will there be lectures, hands-on learning, alternative activities?
Others discuss wanting to ski Mt. Vinson.
Having attained the pole,
the Russians—most who travelled as individuals
but bonded as a group upon arrival—
finally vote *nyet* and opt to leave early,
five days ahead of schedule.
Rajesh also decided to depart with them.

I am the only one left from our group.
If this makes me a misfit
I happily accept being an outlier.
My goals are to rest, move slowly,
do some writing and reading,
observe a plane land,
eat when hungry, attend lectures,
and watch some Antarctic-related films.

My guides will surprise me
with a cross-country skiing trip
leading to a fantasy picnic

some distance from the base camp
where we discovered
brave algae and lichens growing
from the crevice of one of the few visible rocks
(actually the summit of a buried mountain).
Even their two inches of determined growth
took hundreds of years to mature
under such extreme conditions.

Everything takes longer here.
Living out of a backpack
involves a lot of remembering
where everything is, losing it,
and finding it once again.
Life is mired in logistics.

Since my tent-mate accompanied the exodus,
I can now spread out all my gear.
I sleep with ear plugs due to the wind.
At one point I could have sworn
someone was playing a flute
in a nearby tent but surely
fingers would freeze?
The wind section of
a polar orchestra.

IX.

The next morning,
sipping hot oolong tea
and listening to mellow music
from an early iPad hooked up to speakers

in the large dining tent,
I feel refreshed, the harbinger of a new day.
Sure enough, I am welcomed into
a six-wheel-drive, blue Ford SUV,
superbly modified in Iceland,
along with a driver and three staff;
a fivesome joy-riding in a vehicle
that had reached the pole three times
on a seven-day, overland outing
with three people taking turns:
driving, guiding, sleeping.
Far beyond the blue-ice runway,
we venture on a roadless two hour's drive from camp.
It is exhilarating and dangerous.
Just before I left YVR,
I scribbled a quote from Kurt Vonnegut
in my all-weather field book:
"Bizarre travel plans are dancing lessons
from God" and now I could add
"…even in godforsaken places."
Although the essence of all geographies
feels equal to me. Just different.
Unique. Not forsaken at all, especially
in the greater scheme of things
where continents drift like
dust in the wind over the surface of
our pulsating Living Planet.

There is no map to follow, just a compass.
We see mountain peaks framing glaciers
and outcroppings on either side called Elephant Heads.
These marble-like plinths are visible

from several kilometres away.
One serrated peak reminds me of Mount Serrat,
a hermit-and-monastery-laden mountain
I had visited just north of Barcelona.
Agreeing on the similarities,
this peak is now officially named
—by us—as Mount Serrat.
Naming a peak will later give some pleasure
but it feels insignificant at the time.
I am overwhelmed by the glaciers
and miles of imperceptibly moving ice sheets.
Pushed by gravity and ever-moving air,
these great frozen rivers have smothered
entire mountain ranges far below.
It is mystifying and otherworldly.
One soon tires of binocular gazing.
I am more astonished than afraid.

Our Icelandic-outfitted SUV has tires
that cost about $1,000 each.
They can be individually deflated
or inflated to increase or reduce traction.
Made from custom-made rubber compounds,
they remain pliable in freezing temperatures.
The dashboard has so many
switches, dials, buttons and knobs
that it is easy to feel invincible
in a sci-fi kind of way.

X.

Then about an hour from camp

someone thinks they have detected a flat.
No, it is the axle connecting 5 and 6
to the four other wheels at the front.
I find some of the broken parts
scattered a few yards behind us.
We don't have the tools to fix it.
A satellite phone is used to call for help.
Union Glacier Camp responds.
No one panics. We wait in the SUV
with thermos-warmed tea
and chocolate chip cookies.
Restless for some alone time
and drawn to connect
with the venerable fields of ice,
I decide to take a short walk on my own.
Granted permission, I am warned not to stray:
there could be crevices.
Many explorers, their sleds, dogs and vehicles
have been suddenly swallowed by such hidden
denizens of the polar deep.
I put on an extra fleece cap
and wander back down the makeshift road
to create some respectful space between me
and the other humans.
At first, I just stand there,
staring calmly into a distance
that keeps disappearing
beneath the bleached camouflage
of snow on a thousand-mile blanket
of perfectly undisturbed ice.
Then I close my eyes.

Once before, in China, I had done this
on my first night there,
alone in a dark hotel garden.
I'd stood erect, closed my eyes
and imagined how China
had considered itself to be
the Middle Kingdom,
the centre of the earth,
not at all the "East."
And so I had expunged
my Western-centricity.

A year-and-a-half previously,
in the other Land of Eternal Ice,
at the northern axis
of a gently tilting planet,
I laid upon the frozen seas
and contemplated a cosmic vortex
running through Gaia's spine,
as mine.

Now, at the southern terminus of the Polar Express,
I am able to join forces and complete the circuit.
I came to realize that except for purposes
of temporary reference and human conceit,
there is no longer an up or a down.
Standing in the nether south
I am not upside down,
no more than those in the north
are right-side up.
At last, dizzyingly,
my Northern bias expires.

And still,
so still,
I stand at the Pole
of expired desire.

On December 10, 2012, in the South Pole guest book, Yosef Wosk wrote:

What a privilege to join you on this journey to the ends of the Earth! Last year I was fortunate to travel to the North Pole aboard a Russian nuclear-powered icebreaker. The axis of the north and south feel like the Earth's spine, like crown chakra and grounded here through the feet, Keter and Malkhut, theory and manifestation, potential and actualization, dream and awakening, birthing through one dimension and embracing a new—as yet undefined—reality.

There is no longer a need to romanticize a far-off goal. The mundane, everyday, is now sufficient along with a continuous effort to serve others— whether transcendent spirit, nature, people, the moment. The poles are now parentheses and we are its comments.

Thank you to the wonderful staff here at Union Glacier. They served as equals, often fulfilling multiple roles. I have only seen this among Turkish Sufis. "You will be my servant and I will be your slave." So it is in this great continuum from here to eternity. But especially here.

Blessed is the Essence of the Universe who has made the Works of Creation.

When an Inuit hunter spots a herd of caribou, this is the gesture he makes. Curved hands represent antlers, fingers correspond to the number of caribou. One's body is turned in the direction of the prey. Print by Joseph (Eegyvudluk) Pootoogook (1887-1958).

In appreciation of the 1958 print by Joseph Pootoogook: "Joyfully, I see ten caribou."

NORTH POLE

Yosef Wosk has travelled to northern polar regions three times, all aboard Russian vessels. In 2010, he participated in a geographic and educational expedition to the Canadian High Arctic and Greenland aboard the research vessel, Akademik Ioffe. *In 2011, in order to successfully reach the North Pole, he embarked from Murmansk on a nuclear-powered icebreaker* 50 Let Pobedy / 50 Years of Victory, *so-named because it was commissioned fifty years after the victory of WW II. In 2016, as a Fellow of the Royal Canadian Geographical Society, he was a participant in just the eleventh voyage in history to attempt a circumnavigation of the Arctic Ocean. This third expedition aboard the venerable* Kapitan Khlebnikov *icebreaker succeeded in transiting the Northeast Passage over Russia, completing the Northwest Passage over Canada, and exiting through the Bering Strait, but it failed to complete the first circumnavigation of Greenland due to extreme weather. Wosk's second Arctic expedition would prove the most alarming. The threatening wonder of the natural world beyond his state room sometimes felt less hazardous than the psychological atmosphere aboard the vessel. — Ed.*

THERE IS AN OLD SAYING that I just made up: "Every detour leads to your true destination." I had to travel to the ends of the Earth to discover not just the frozen polar regions but also some frigid regions of the heart.

I, like millions before me, imagined travelling to the North Pole but never thought that I could go that far. As I got older, and as my travels encompassed much of the world, I gradually began stretching towards the final frontier. At first it seemed impossible. Such expeditions were for governments or explorers, for researchers or madmen.

But my travels crept progressively north, seduced by the curve of the planet, until one day I woke up to the possibility of crossing yet another horizon and being at the still, turning point of the world.

Of course, all this begins with our inheritance of human consciousness, with our urge to know both the outer and the inner limits of everything that exists. How tall is that mountain, how deep the sea; how fast can I run, how far can I fall? How unobtainable is infinity, how near is now?

After a year of investigation, I found the company and the ship that would sail north from Russia towards the coveted journey's end. It felt like such a private, forbidden appetite that I had to whisper the idea even to myself and only revealed my plans to others who had to know to where I was eloping.

Ten months before the voyage, I registered for a double cabin on what turned out to be the world's most powerful nuclear-fueled icebreaker, the Russian vessel *50 Years of Victory*. I had been divorced for a number of years and assumed one of my children might want to make the trip. I had already travelled with my son, Avi, to the highest and lowest places on Earth—Mount Everest and the Dead Sea—as well as to Asia, Antarctica and the Arctic. I'd also travelled extensively with my daughters, Rahel and Shevi, mainly in Canada, the United States, Europe, the Caribbean and Israel. It turned out that my daughters were both preoccupied with their budding relationships and Avi was newly committed to the Pacific Institute of Culinary Arts where he was training as a chef.

I had often travelled alone. I told myself I could do it once more. But

I still felt such a momentous experience would best be fulfilled with a companion: someone with whom I could review the daily adventures and prepare for tours; someone who would not be a stranger in an otherwise unknown land; a companion so we could support one another when difficulties might inevitably arise and perhaps even share some intimacy.

I tried to ignore the voice inside my head that said, "You really *should* be with someone." I told myself I could not dare hope for romance to bloom in the few months remaining before my departure. I had recently been attracted to a woman I met at a book fair in San Francisco, but when I gently broached the subject of travel, I discovered she got seasick and couldn't abide long sea voyages.

It wouldn't be right to ask a stranger anyway, so I naturally thought of Heather, originally from Australia and now living in the ancient port of Jaffa. We had travelled to the Australian outback and walked for hours in Dreamtime, around Uluru, the great Red Rock at the navel of the distant continent. She was an adventurous spirit by nature. We were compatible. We both liked to laugh and our relationship had ended respectfully and amicably. It would have been inappropriate, however, to offer an abrupt invitation to a grand adventure, unbidden.

Then, out of the blue, I appeared in one of Maddy's dreams. About six months before my scheduled departure, she contacted me, asking if we might consider another rendezvous. Madelaine and I had known each other in various contexts for about seven years but we had never been a couple. Two years had passed since I'd seen her. She lived across the border, about a three-hour drive away. She was a therapist and a musician, and I had been intrigued that she felt inspired by the biblical prophet and music-maker, Miriam. She had been newly divorced when we met and she had retained her independence. We visited one another a couple of promising times a few years before and had exchanged emails for a few months.

Maddy knew nothing about my Arctic plans but after we reconnected, I picked up the phone and took the plunge. I asked her if she would like to accompany me on this extraordinary journey to the Far North. She thought about it overnight and happily accepted the invitation the next day with a sense of anxious gratitude.

Once more we spent an exploratory weekend together, subtly testing our interests, how we got along and our physical attraction to one another. We were both careful not to cross any unspoken, untrusted borders. There were respectful but not ravenous kisses. Looking over the 49th parallel, it looked like a favourable fit.

She shared some tentative reservations about a number of issues such as her weak knees, her fear that I might back out, our level of intimacy, and her inexperience in travel, but otherwise she accepted the adventure in a promising way. I explained there would be two separate beds. It was understood that we could be amorous—or not. It is easy to say now that it should have been more openly discussed. Then again, romance beckons when the future is unknown.

Over the next few months—with the assistance of Quark Expeditions and Tanya, our trusted, formerly Ukrainian, travel agent—we prepared for the epic northern pilgrimage. The voyage to and from the Pole would take two weeks but since we were already travelling so far from home, I arranged for preliminary visits to Moscow and St. Petersburg. From there we would take the train to Helsinki, in Finland. and then a ferry across the Gulf of Finland, an arm of the Baltic Sea, to visit Tallin in Estonia, a fascinating combination of medieval "Old Town" and high-tech modern city.

Upon returning from the Pole, we would spend a few days in London with its wonderful museums, theatres, bookstores, restaurants and shops. From there, we would take adjacent excursions to prehistoric Stonehenge, the pomp of Windsor Castle and the healing town of Bath. The *planned* trip, with its numerous arrangements and tens of harbours, was a great success-in-the-making. The *actual* journey, however, presented unforeseen emotional challenges.

After months of research, meetings, phone calls and countless emails, Tanya sent a complete set of documents to both of us—the full itinerary, tickets, all the logistics and many contact numbers. In confidence, she mentioned to me that she was surprised by Madelaine's reaction. Instead of expressing thanks, Maddy had admonished the travel agent by saying that she herself was very well-organized, she didn't need all those documents and that she already had everything in order.

When we reached St. Petersburg, prior to setting sail, we went for a long walk in a gentle rain in search of a particular kosher restaurant. We walked for an hour, ostensibly as happy as could be. She had the map in her hands. Seemingly, we were on an amicable adventure in a beautiful place until she admitted she could not read the street signs in Russian Cyrillic script. I was able to translate them for several course corrections. As I did so, I realized that my ability would nonetheless not prevent us from getting lost and this did *not* appeal to her.

When you are in a foreign place, out of your comfort zone, tempers can flare more easily. I was told that even if I could read the signs, I still had a terrible sense of direction. That's how I discovered she was someone who needed to feel she was in charge; she had to make herself the authority on nearly every subject, even if it was obvious that she had no idea what she was talking about. Maddy remained a vivacious and attractive personality, with a vibrant mind, but I had to hold my tongue a dozen times so as not to be drawn into conflict.

Having had diabetes for about five years, I could be affected by low or high blood sugar. The following night, when we were again searching for a restaurant, as travellers do, uncertain when faced with a barrage of options and unknowns, we could not reach a consensus and I simply asserted that I needed to eat and there was a good-looking Italian restaurant across the street, the da Vinci. We had dinner there, one of the best plates of spaghetti I'd tasted outside of Napoli. As soon as the meal was done, Maddy announced she was tired and was going back to the hotel to rest and sleep.

I wanted to go for a walk and headed off, without a destination. I followed some others to a park under the spire of the Admiralty about a block away. There was a large circular fountain, songbirds perched in broad leaf trees, sculptures of authors and composers, the high summer sun of a white northern night, the soundscape a mixture of all ages, and the echo of music in the background, which I thought might be buskers. I sat down, relaxed, and became filled with gratitude, an attitude that blossomed into a profound spiritual state of well-being.

Eventually, I slowly followed the ever-louder music until I was surprised to see crowds and jumbo screens across the broad Russian boulevard. This was the Sting concert that our guide had hinted at earlier but I thought was being held at an indoor arena on the other side of town. Intuitive meandering had led me here, and as I half-levitated my way into the crowd I could hear Sting's unmistakable voice: "Don't stand, don't stand, don't stand so close to me."

Exhaustion finally guided me back to the hotel where I was keen to share news of my serendipitous discovery. When I entered the lobby, I was surprised to see Maddy on a bench, tapping on her computer, looking not the least bit fatigued. When I greeted her, she resented my interruption, so I kept my distance. Still feeling euphoric, I eventually quietly told her about my evening stroll and the accidental Sting concert. Contrite, she soon went out for a walk of her own. I soon fell into a deep but conflicted sleep.

Anyone who has travelled a lot knows it's important to cut one's travel companion some slack. The strain of crossing so many time zones can play havoc on the best of us. Sure enough, by the time we reached our embarkation point at Murmansk, we had been intimate a few times. I was optimistic. I hoped heading towards the North Pole, sharing a grand adventure, would eventually bring us even closer together.

But as we sailed to and from the North Pole, I sometimes perceived our boat, like a metaphor for our planet, to be a Ship of Fools. The interaction of couples, though often filled with love and laughter, was also frequently characterized by tension, unhappiness and arguments. I witnessed the remote looks in their sad eyes as they negotiated and compromised, made arrangements and set meetings that resulted in a loss of liberty. Those wounded wanderers tended to trade freedom for servitude, silence for too many words, and spontaneity for an agenda set long ago in a corporate board room.

Murmansk, with a population of more than 300,000, is the world's largest city north of the Arctic Circle. Situated on the far northwest coast of Russia, it is the homeport of *RosAtomFlot* [Russian Atomic Fleet] and headquarters of the Russian Northern Navy.

Even after the 1991 collapse of the Soviet Union and expectations of extensive democratic reforms, Russia still often feels like a country under siege. Although it is by far the largest country in the world (at over 6,600,000 square miles it is twice the size of Canada) it still suffers from xenophobic paranoia. Security is very tight and travel visas are often difficult to obtain. If it were not for the tourist and commercial dollars that help buoy the economy, the borders would be sealed even tighter.

Russia's settlement of the Arctic region is more pronounced than any of the seven other countries within the Arctic Circle including Norway, Sweden, Iceland, Finland, Canada, United States [Alaska] and Denmark [Greenland]. Russia has more towns, a greater population (of over two million people) and more industrial, economic and military development in the polar north than the rest of the world combined. This will only increase as global warming results in much less or even no Arctic ice at all. Sailing from East Asia to Europe via the Northeast Passage over Russia, rather than having to take the southern route through the Suez Canal, will reduce the time by at least forty percent fewer days at sea. This will be a huge commercial incentive.

The brochure for our North Pole trip announced it with these dramatic words: "The World's Most Exclusive Arctic Expedition. You could be one of only 128 people in the Universe who will sail to the top of the world in 2011."

Our ship, *50 Years of Victory,* was the largest and strongest nuclear-powered icebreaker in the world. Driven by two nuclear reactors that produce up to 75,000 hp, it is 524 feet long and 98 feet wide. It can remain at sea for almost eight months and its nuclear fuel only needs to be replaced every four years. By the end of our two-week, 3,000-mile expedition, instead of burning 1,000 tons of heavy duty marine-grade oil, the ship used about a kilogram of uranium fuel and emitted no significant quantity of greenhouse gas. Of course, disposing of the spent uranium at a later date remains a delicate and somewhat controversial procedure.

50 Years of Victory was twenty years in the making. It was planned to be launched in 1995, to mark the fifty years since the end of the Second World War and the Russian victory over Germany in the Great Patriotic War. However, the chaos following the breakup of the Soviet Union, followed by a fire in the shipyard, delayed its commission until 2007. It was the first Arktika-class icebreaker to have a spoon-shaped bow, capable of breaking through ice up to 2.8 meters (9.2 feet) thick. Contrary to popular opinion, icebreakers do not ram their way through ice, forcing it to crack from horizontal pressure, but rather use a combination of forces, predominantly that of bearing down upon the ice-thickened seas with the weight of their double-hulled, steel reinforced bow.

Icebreakers attempt to follow open leads in the ice and navigate through paths of least resistance. Satellite technology has greatly enhanced this surveillance. Even so, the mighty ship occasionally came up against impassible barriers known as pressure ridges. On these occasions, the captain would follow one of two tactics: Either put the vessel in reverse for a few hundred metres and then ram forward with a determined blow, or reverse and search for a more amenable opening in the frozen waters, even if it involved a significant detour.

Victory and its sister ships are painted with a black hull and a bright international orange superstructure to make it more visible amidst the surrounding polar ocean and icescape. This is important for rescue missions in case of mechanical failures.

Originally built to clear a path through icebound waters for cargo ships following behind, or for scientific research or covert military purposes, the interior of *Victory* was later retrofitted to accommodate about 120 passengers for tourist cruises and to attract much-needed foreign currency for the Russian economy. The crew, from the captain to the kitchen staff, ranges from approximately 130 to over 200.

Our polar cruise was organized by a travel company that chartered the great ship from the Russian government. They provided all logistics and programs including a leader, guides, excursions, special programs and a full schedule of informative lectures by an assorted staff of international experts including a geologist, geographer, glaciologist, historian, biologist, ornithologist, and daily briefings from our expedition leader.

Excellent meals, always with a choice of menu and themed daily specials, were served in a dedicated dining room. Those who favoured alcohol were liberally supplied. Snacks were regularly available and afternoon tea, featuring fresh warm pastries, was welcomed. It was a comfortable but certainly not a luxurious cruise. Everyone pitched in to the best of their ability. Most were dedicated travellers on the trip of a lifetime safely ensconced in the buoyant metal ark. As for me, I was in geographic heaven.

There were various cabin configurations: Maddy's and my room contained two beds, a desk and chair, a small closet, a modest bathroom with a shower in which there was hardly enough room to turn around, and two portholes that opened to let in fresh sea air. One had to remember, however, to lock them during turbulent days at sea. Room doors were never locked when we were out of the rooms. This somewhat surprising policy—one that aroused initial feelings of suspicion from this security-conscious city dweller—served a number of functions, mostly relating to safety.

Before settling in, we were instructed to meet on deck, at the Muster Stations, for an emergency drill in case of any disasters such as a fire, collision, or a problem with the nuclear reactors. The ship carried covered lifeboats hoisted on cranes and equipped with provisions. We were assigned our numbered boats, crawled inside for a few moments to familiarize ourselves with how they worked, and were assured that we could survive floating in the frozen waters until rescued within a few hours or in a couple of days.

Victory carried an eight-passenger helicopter for shore excursions to otherwise unreachable areas and for flights over the vast icefields surrounding our ship. The onboard helicopter also assisted the captain with ice navigation and reconnaissance. It was kept tied down on a helipad on the back deck.

The ship also had a number of Zodiac boats aboard. These are small inflatable craft with an outboard motor that are typically used for ship-to-shore landings or short exploratory trips among fields of ice. Due to hazardous ice conditions and only one landing opportunity between Murmansk and the Pole, no Zodiac excursions were offered on this trip.

We did, however, have one helicopter expedition. That landing was in Franz Josef Land, Eurasia's northernmost landmass. Nine hundred miles northeast of Murmansk and just over 600 miles south of the Pole, it consists of an archipelago of 191 flat-topped islands of varying sizes with steep basalt cliffs. No Indigenous population lives there; its only human inhabitants are Russian scientists and military personnel. It was the only landmass we would see on the entire trip as we sailed for two weeks through the Arctic Ocean.

It was during this portion of the journey that I took note of a quotation credited to an obscure author named Marie Le Fort:

After all, you need to be a bit possessed,

do you not, to journey to the ends of the earth,
finding nourishment in the sole idea of voyage?

As we were returning to *Victory* after that stopover in Cape Flora, Franz Josef Land, some of us were nearly seriously injured when birds collided with our helicopter's rotors. The helicopter shuddered, lurched to its side and dropped before the pilot was able to bring it back under control just before hitting the water. He was able to get us back to the island for an emergency landing.

While the pilot eventually dared to return alone to the ship with the Sikorsky for repairs [it was grounded for the rest of the trip], we remained distressed and stranded on Cape Flora. We began to prepare ourselves to spend the night alone, with no shelter or food, on a desolate Arctic island. Although we put on brave faces, our minds began to flood with worst case scenarios. Radio contact was eventually made with the ship, however, and a few hours later a small rescue craft picked us up from a rocky landing. Relieved that we had survived a near disaster and celebrating our rescue, we were rewarded with a late supper of hot soup, broad bread and extra rations of vodka.

The bridge, or pilothouse, on the top deck of *Victory* was almost always open so we could observe the ship's navigational instruments, speak with a commanding officer, and get a bird's-eye view of the horizon. There was an adjacent radio and communications room from where it was possible—after some technicalities and paying a considerable fee—to call anywhere in the world. Sometimes it worked but not always and one had to make another appointment with the Communications Officer as he arranged for a channel to transmit and receive signals passing through a satellite orbiting high above the earth. I used the satellite phone once: It was to congratulate my son for graduating as a chef and to tell him that I had successfully reached the North Pole. His graduating, after years of personal turmoil, was his polar achievement.

The ship also had a large meeting room where everyone could assemble, a small clinic, a basic gym, a bar and lounge, as well as a sauna and a saltwater pool (used almost exclusively by the crew) that sloshed over its inadequate confines as the boat continuously shifted in the undulating seas. It was emptied during storms.

A few days into the voyage, a tour of the ship's mechanics was offered to those who were curious. We descended on a series of narrow steel stairways to the lower two decks where we were shown the nuclear reactors, a bank of sophisticated computers and a further suite of engine rooms. Given the general Russian attitude that tends towards high levels of national security, I was surprised we were permitted to view the nuclear technology. I left feeling impressed with Russian ingenuity and optimistic about their friendliness. I wished that a greater degree of ongoing trust and cooperation existed between us.

Meanwhile, back above board, the bow and stern as well as multiple levels of outdoor walkways were frequently visited to breathe the pristine invigorating air, absorb the unending panorama and take photographs of nature's beauty.

The further north we travelled, the thicker the sea ice became. The rumbling of the great Leviathan-as-ship crushing through the frozen ocean sent shudders along her hull. The vibrations may have frightened some passengers, but I welcomed them as a reassuring encounter with the resisting icescape and as a steady baritone chorus, a visceral indication that we had entered the polar seas. After all, we were the alien species forcing our way among her virgin waters. I only wanted to sail on with as much respect as possible for this habitat.

Even as we fractured the ice, the break proved temporary because the ocean currents and Arctic air soon began to mend the tear behind us. Standing on the rearward stern, one could witness the tactile waters, as nature's tailor, stitching the frozen wound back together.

As for stormy seas: We travelled during the Arctic summer when the incessant sunshine thaws the upper ice covering the ocean and calms the winds. The captain followed multiple weather reports in an effort to navigate through the most tranquil waters but there was some occasional rocking and rolling, as in the Barents Sea, when the tempest picked up and the ocean swells awoke.

Victory was equipped with sophisticated stabilizing technology that compensated for such disturbances and maintained a relatively even keel, but passengers were reminded to keep one hand for themselves and one for the ship. We felt confident with the strength of our vessel. I have, however, been on other ships, larger or smaller, that were buffeted by storms and resulted in broken arms, gashed heads and other injuries, to say nothing of debilitating *mal de mer,* seasickness. And who could forget the unsinkable *Titanic,* just over a century ago, fatally ripped apart by an iceberg a few hundred miles away.

There are so many kinds of ice that we even had a glaciologist aboard to offer lectures on the topic. We learned to identify icebergs: floating with ninety percent of their mass below the ocean's surface, they are composed entirely of fresh water. Smaller chunks of frozen sea water take various forms of pack ice. There are over fifty terms to describe types and stages of ice, including some with colourful names such as bergy bits, brash ice, hummock and bummock, blue ice, floeburg, frazil ice, glaze and grease ice, growlers, nilas, nipped and pancake ice, tabular, tongue, and sastrugi.

The Arctic, a world unto its own, also boasts unique atmospheric phenomena such as the *Aurora Borealis* (the Northern Lights) and the sundog, a rainbow halo around the sun. Since it was summer and we were bathed in 24-hour sunlight, the *Aurora* was not visible but I did witness a couple of stunning sundogs over the frigid Arctic seas.

Those who have not travelled to the polar regions may assume they are too cold to support life, but land, sea and air are filled with seasonal bounty. Since our expedition was a journey into the Arctic wilderness where human civilization had not yet imposed its ubiquitous will, nature was the featured attraction. We spent days with our binoculars and telephoto camera lenses observing the manifestation of the Great Mother.

The overwhelming presence of humanity, so evident in southern settlements, was replaced with a sense of peaceful equanimity; the urgency of unrelenting time was substituted with the vastness of unending space. It was as if there was one day of work and six days of Sabbath, though the reality of survival in the polar desert is a full-time and often harrowing job. As a result of these profound engagements, my perception shifted from placing human drama at the centre of attention to substituting it for the unfolding of nature, a shift from *egocentric* to *ecocentric* consciousness.

We learned to identify Arctic birds either flying in flocks or occasional lone birds in search of a meal or blown off course by wayward winds. Some travellers kept a log of their sightings but since no one could chance to see them all, a cumulative list was posted on the bridge. Some winged wonders ventured far off over the open ocean while others kept closer to land. Instead of Fords, Chevys and Hondas, there were the fulmar, kittiwake, little auk and various guillemots (which looked like flying penguins). On the flat tundra, nest species such as the common eider, purple sandpiper, Arctic skua, glaucous gull, ivory gull, Arctic tern and snow bunting appeared.

Marine mammals included polar bear and walrus, harp seal and bearded seal, as well as rare sightings of humpback and bowhead whales. (On other trips to Arctic regions, I encountered musk ox, Arctic fox and white wolf, reindeer, snowy owl, falcon and eagle, Arctic hare, ermine, lemming and vole as well as narwhal—the "unicorns of the sea"—and pods of white beluga whales.)

The sea beneath us teemed with fish, many of which have evolved to produce anti-freeze proteins to help keep them warm enough to thrive in the cold. Life on the seafloor is similarly prolific.

The scarf that I wore on this voyage, purchased on a previous odyssey to Greenland, was woven from musk ox wool called *qiviut* in Inuit. It is taken from the downy undercoat of the musk ox, an animal that is actually a magnificent type of prehistoric goat that lives in the northern Arctic regions. *Qiviut* is a lightweight fibre, softer than cashmere and eight times warmer than sheep's wool. Since musk ox are not domesticated, these fibres are collected from the bushes and tundra where the animals naturally shed.

Finally, after seven days and nights at sea, we reached our destination at the height of the Arctic summer. The temperature was a balmy -10° C. After celebrating with fellow passengers and crew, I wandered off to spend some hermetic time on my own.

Since I was wrapped so densely in insulating layers of clothing, I could not comfortably sit on the frozen ice suspended upon the northern sea. I therefore lay on my back, arms and legs serenely outstretched like a human antenna, and surrendered myself to the void.

At first, I was concerned that someone may have thought I had fainted, and sure enough Maddy sent someone over to check on me after a few moments. By that point I was beyond communicating with words but did manage to grunt a polite "uh huh" when questioned if I was okay.

Although I needed others to fulfill my isolated goal, my only desire was to now withdraw into a private polar nirvana. My body gradually relaxed, breath slowed, thoughts disappeared. I let the experience take me away. I became electrified, the nexus of an energy surge. I opened to a vertical axis of energetic consciousness that originated in the limitless sky above, entered through my navel and continued deep into the Earth before exiting at the South Pole and continuing its cosmic journey beyond. It was such an all-consuming reverie that it would take me months to share it with even one other person.

On my back, like some marooned sapien seal, I was seized by this unanticipated epiphany of transcendent unity. I reflected how the planet is a friend, an ally, our home and host. It feeds and nourishes us, supports and protects us. It is precious beyond measure. We are an ephemeral species. One day we will vanish but today we ennoble our existence and live for one another. I partnered the earth, took the planet in my arms and danced with eternity. The North was worth all the difficulties after all.

From the North Pole, every direction is south. Having reached the top of the world, there is no one above us. It was an exhilarating feeling to contemplate that my head now swayed among the stars. On one hand, we generally feel protected by the earth's enveloping atmosphere, and yet that also produces a subconscious opposite reaction of wanting to be liberated from the planet's prison. Attaining the Pole fulfilled that visceral desire.

I have never felt so free.

Arctic sailors have a saying: "When you're at the North Pole, the whole world is at your feet." Few people get to feel the earth that way. Travelling either by foot and sled, airplane, balloon, surface ship or submarine, only a few thousand people have arrived at the geographic zenith of our world since it was first achieved over a century ago.

After centuries of failed attempts and lost lives, the first ship to reach the North Pole was the Russian nuclear-powered icebreaker *Arktika* in August 1977, just thirty-four years before our own voyage. The first group of paying passengers to reach the Pole aboard a converted research icebreaker, via the Northeast Passage and across the Russian Arctic, did so only twenty years before us. By 2011, we were among the first eighty ships to have ever arrived at 90° North.

Only a few hundred tourists have traveled to *both* the North and South Poles. In theory, one can even visit both Poles in the same year since the polar regions are opposite one another: the Antarctic summer begins on December 21st while the Arctic Summer Solstice is on July 21st. However, it is likely that only a few dozen tourists have visited both poles in the same year.

My expeditions to both poles would be separated by 17 months: the North Pole in July 2011, followed by the South Pole in December 2012.

After reaching the Pole, the icebreaker fired up its nuclear reactors and headed in the only direction it could, South, and I would discover that the most arduous part of the journey was just beginning.

Throughout my nautical adventure aboard the good ship *Victory*, there was a parallel Journey of the Heart unfolding in Cabin B49 that was just as daunting. I was discovering a different type of ice.

We sailed for another seven days on the return voyage to Murmansk with only one planned stop at the soaring Gibraltar-like Rubini Rock on Franz Josef Land, the home of large bird rookeries and occasional polar bear sightings. The captain manoeuvred the great ship to within a few yards of the massive rock as tens of thousands of nesting sea birds swirled around us to the clatter of clicking cameras and a symphony of muted oohs and aahs. This was appropriate because the almost unbroken squawking of the cliff-dwelling avians was named in 1895 for Giovanni Rubini, an Italian opera singer.

Meanwhile, it became increasingly difficult for Maddy and me to carry on an extended conversation. When I would say something, share a thought, offer an opinion, point something out, or state a matter of fact, Maddy would almost always answer in a way that "transferred" or "arrogated" whatever I said towards her own field of imagined authority or experience. Perhaps that is relatively normal, perhaps not. Either way, I felt I could no longer communicate with her.

I was cloistered for another ten days with my unpredictable and distressed travelling companion until we returned to North America. Although there were still some fine moments, the emotional conditions for Maddy and me continued to deteriorate. Our time together on the return voyage was more generally characterized by intolerable silence, arguments and a longing to extricate ourselves from the social contract. Instead of laughter and sexual intimacy, I fantasized about having a large order of fish & chips with a cold beer at Doc Morgan's Pub on Bowen Island.

There I was, the ersatz explorer, a far cry from being a psychiatrist; and yet, somehow, I had to come to terms with the fact that I had reached the top of the earth only to fall to the nadir of manhood in the form of a jilted lover. Has anyone ever written a travel article along these lines? The perils of incompatibility? In cramped quarters? Past middle age?

If not, somebody ought to, I thought. Blaming only Madelaine would have been far too easy; too much of a knee-jerk reaction like the first man, Adam, and the first woman, Eve, in the perfect garden planted to the east of Eden. Defensively concealing themselves in the shadows, each one blamed the other but, in the end, both were exiled.

We are in constant negotiation with various aspects of our many minds, hence I do have some appreciation for the complexity of human consciousness, but only later did it dawn on me that Maddy had different overt personalities. From day to day, hour to hour, and minute to minute, I did not know which one of her would show up: Madelaine or one of her opposites, whom I'll call Sybil.

The former, authoritarian personality knew everything; Sybil, the latter, couldn't decide what to eat, if to eat at all, let alone what to wear, where to go, how long to stay, what to buy and tens of other debilitating choices. With either personality, the emotional payoff seemed to be in the conflict, not in the resolution. Who knows; perhaps she thought the same about me.

I gradually began to develop sympathy for her. How could she be with me if she was already in a wrestling match within? Everything for Sybil became a personal conundrum. When I once asked her about this trait of indecisiveness, she defended it by saying that she liked to live in the moment. I agreed that there were times to live in the moment, but she was not yet a Taoist or Zen master. I now wish I had found a more tactful response.

We both suffered humiliation at each other's hands. She said some very unpleasant things. In retaliation, I told her how I felt caught in a pincer movement between her two personalities: one demanding to lead, to be the dominant personality, the other unsure where we were, diametrically opposed to the powerful, assertive and controlling one. I let her have her say, her opinion, her way, in an effort to maintain the peace, but my tongue was covered with metaphorical scars for the number of times that I bit it to avoid getting into an argument.

We tried to give one another as much space and time as possible so as not to feel claustrophobic. There were times when it seemed more appropriate to wait a few moments and go together or, conversely, to strike out on our own. I saved her seats often, and when she did show up, she never liked the ones I had chosen.

Eventually it was easier, on both of us, if I simply took care of myself. Towards the end of our trip, in London, it became impossible to retain equilibrium. Maddy got angry any number of times for petty or imaginary trespasses. Once, not far from Big Ben and Westminster Abbey, after less than a minute's discussion, she put up her fists and shouted at me: "You want to hit me? Go ahead and hit me! Hit me!"

That is when I turned on my heels and got out of her presence as fast as I could. I realized with alarm that there was some old pattern emerging in which I didn't want to get trapped. I remembered her telling me in the past that she had once challenged her father with those identical words.

This new predicament felt every bit as distressing as finding myself stuck on that Arctic island, stranded, left behind after the helicopter had nearly crashed and we were abandoned, with night approaching, after the pilot had bravely flown back to the ship for repairs.

If we could not have tenderness I thought, perhaps naively, we could compensate ourselves with honesty. I wanted our post-Arctic encounters to be a learning experience, an effort to repair and redeem ourselves, a return to the garden, if only to pull a few painful weeds.

But, sadly, it was not to be.

When I tried to broach the subject of an earlier psychological trauma, I was shot down in flames, until finally we boarded the return flight home. Strapped in our seats, hardly a word was spoken for the next ten detached hours, the opposite of how we began our promising journey one long month ago.

When she later trusted me enough to share some of her fears, and I could more fully appreciate her struggles, it helped me to accept our situation and gradually put my mind at rest about our precarious voyage.

Here are some excerpts from a much longer letter sent after our voyage.

Madelaine,

I've been thinking of writing to you ever since we returned home. It is now three weeks although it feels like three months. I had to wait for some objectivity to set in.

This message is sent with care. In the larger picture, we are both dedicated to a life of introspection, growth, personal development and higher consciousness.

I want to thank you for travelling with me. It was a month long intensive series of experiences, both geographic and emotional. We both took significant risks.

I will treasure those times when we were being open and kind with one another. I will never forget when you "came for a visit" between the chasm of our twin beds in Moscow. Please accept these soul-soaked words as a farewell.

Yosef

Such is the logbook of a contemporary explorer.

Since then, I've embarked on other journeys. These have included a four-month cruise around the world and my subsequent expedition deep into the interior of the Antarctic culminating with vodka drunk with more Russians at the sister South Pole. I sometimes still travel with a friend on shorter excursions but my difficult experience with Maddy has served to wean me from the social conformity of travelling with a companion for longer expeditions. I have since observed others travelling alone, either because of cost or predilection, and I have watched travelling—not necessarily vacationing—couples interact. Some shared joy, laughter, conversation, supporting and loving together. But others clearly did not. There is no right way, there is no wrong way; there is only the way.

Madelaine is not her real name. I have since discovered the following quote by Theodore Isaac Rubin and thought it appropriate, not only in my case but for most of us:

I must learn to love the fool in me—the one who feels too much, talks too much, takes too many chances, wins sometimes and loses often, lacks self-control, loves and hates, hurts and gets hurt, promises and breaks promises, laughs and cries. It alone protects me against that utterly self-controlled, masterful tyrant whom I also harbor and who would rob me of human aliveness, humility, and dignity but for my fool.

An enormous, painted Buddhist prayer wheel at a mountain shrine in Bhutan, 2010.

FOOL'S JOURNEY

*I have always felt like a fool, somewhat awkward in an unfamiliar world—
as if I had just awakened from a distant dream and been planted, like
Adam, in a strange Garden of Gaia. I spent most of my life as an unrepen-
tant pilgrim, exploring often exotic and embarrassing sensations of mind,
body and soul. I judged myself as others judged me and sought the safety
of solitude in the far corners of the earth. These are some reflections on my
travels. I have witnessed ancient wonders, been caressed by the breathless
breeze, and deeply humbled by near-death experiences from which I am
grateful to have survived. Sharing these stories is not a boast but an obligation. Becoming a storyteller—sometimes in the haunted guise of an Ancient
Mariner—is the price the cosmos exacts for having encountered its secret
self. Be well, be wild, be wise. — Y.W.*

I SHALL NEVER FORGET OUR APPROACH to Paro, the only international
airport in Bhutan. The airline was Drukair (Dragon Air), Royal Bhutan
Airlines, Flight A319. The plane was flown by one of only eight pilots
qualified to land there: a retired British Airways pilot who had to severe-
ly tilt the wings on our approach through a narrow opening between
deep valleys and 18,000-foot misted mountains. With no radar to guide
planes to this high-altitude destination that is visible only moments be-

fore landing, and its short runway of only 7,000 feet, the Bhutanese airport is considered one of the most challenging landings in the world. Only daylight approaches in clear weather are permitted; anything else would be disastrous.

One of the many marvels of Bhutan was visiting a Buddhist prayer wheel, or mantra mill in a mountain shrine. Inscribed on its exterior was the mantra *Om mani padre hum*, the "Jewel is in the Lotus." It was filled with countless mantras and other spiritual texts printed on cloth or paper and wrapped around the central core; the Tree of Life. Each rotation rings a bell, something that helps count the turns, harmonizes disparate realities, dispels distractions and focuses the mind. Every spin is believed to distribute merit for well-being into the world. This is similar to Tibetan "prayer flags" that disseminate good will and compassion as they flutter in gusts of spirited air.

Only slightly less nerve-wracking than my Drukair experiences were the helicopter excursions from the stern of a Russian nuclear-powered icebreaker and some landings and take-offs aboard an Ilyushin-76 transport plane. The latter was designed in 1967 to deliver heavy machinery to remote areas of the USSR. Our plane had been stolen by the captain and crew during the chaos that followed the collapse of the Soviet Union. That plane's architecture, power and history were as captivating as the four-and-a-half hours it took us to fly from Chile to the heart of Antarctica where we landed on a natural, blue ice runway.

One learns to adapt, by necessity. On my return trip from the Canadian High Arctic, I waited at Kangerlussuaq airport in Greenland for our leased plane, an early model Boeing 727, that was flying up from Tennessee. When we were finally strapped in for take-off, we were informed that because of the lack of sufficient engine thrust and the relatively short runway, the plane was too heavy to take off into the strong wind. Half of us volunteered to get off the aircraft and spend an additional day in Greenland. I volunteered to wait.

Almost all my travels have been explorations, not vacations. To undertake travel to so many out-of-the-way places, one simply must accept an element of risk, whether it's roaming dimly lit caves in Tibet, or trusting taxi drivers in darkened streets when there is no common language. I've rented a room from someone standing around the train station in Communist-era Prague and I've stayed in cheap youth hostels and one-night hotels, not always on the best side of town. My favourite name for a hotel where I stayed is the Yak & Yeti in Kathmandu.

During visits to about one hundred and fifty countries, states, provinces and territories, as well as over a thousand cities, I've also slept in bus, train and police stations; in cars, buses and airports; in the desert and on the street, on benches and beaches, in parks and gardens, in temples and graveyards, in libraries, offices and on porches to escape stifling heat only to be attacked by vampire mosquitoes. I have been roused by beating drums, clanging bells, blaring horns, melodious chants, silent meditations and spinning prayer wheels. I've sat with shamans, chiefs and native priests; endured sweat lodges, meditated in Zendos and been to tea ceremonies among masters in China and Japan. I have often imagined life as a monk in some remote monastery, burning incense at revered shrines, observing prostrations, divinations, benedictions and invocations.

When I was younger and living under the illusion of immortality, I often took chances, but when I became a father, I had to consider that I was also responsible for others. Therefore, for about four decades now, I have decidedly not been a thrill seeker. Only one exception comes to mind. That was the time I was persuaded to be strapped into a body harness attached to a customized parachute called a parasail, then lifted 400 feet behind a speeding boat in Labadee, Haiti. The blast of warm, Caribbean air was invigorating and the view was spectacular if dizzying, but I was mostly relieved when I didn't end up seeing the inside of a Haitian hospital.

Of High Places and Sacred Sites

Some trips can be experimentally high in other ways. On a beach off the road from Pafos to Limassol, in southern Cyprus, a friend and I took LSD at the fabled birthplace of Aphrodite. The beach was gravel and the waters rough but as the long, foaming waters born of the massive surf around the Rock reached the shore, one could easily imagine the earth being impregnated by the semen-bubbled surf and picture the goddess of love emerging from the sea.

While studying for three years in New York, in the late 1970s, I naturally visited sites such as the Statue of Liberty, the Art Deco architectural masterpiece of the Chrysler Building, as well as the Washington Monument obelisk in nearby Washington, D.C., but these were overshadowed—in both height and memory—by my visit to what was the world's tallest building, for nearly forty years, from 1931 to 1970.

Early on the morning of April 8, 1981, we made exceptional arrangements to gain access to the outdoor observation deck of the Empire State Building. In Jewish lore, a traditional blessing is recited when the sun completes its solar cycle once every twenty-eight years on a Tuesday at sundown. When the sun completes this cycle, it has returned to the same position where it was when the world was created.

As we stood to pray, we greeted the sunrise in a celebration of *Birkhat Ha'Hama*, the Blessing of the Sun. From that prominent point, high above one of the great cities in world history, we would be among the first on the continent to view the sun's rebirth.

As an artist, my sister was later part of a group show that was exhibited on the Observatory Level of the World Trade Center before both towers were destroyed by terrorists on September 11, 2001. After the attacks, I undertook a kind of secular pilgrimage to Ground Zero in 2014. I took my family to see the evocative National September 11 Memorial & Museum and the new Freedom Tower, aka One World Trade Center—designed to be the tallest building in the Western Hemisphere. As I write

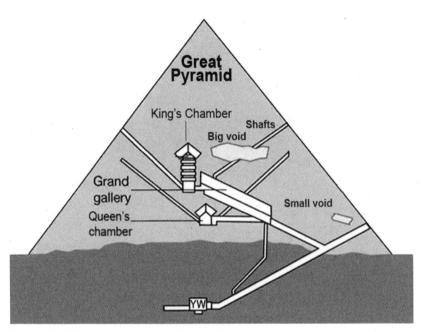

For details of this excursion, see the title piece, Naked in a Pyramid.

this, it is currently the seventh-tallest building in the world at 1,776 feet, a height that recognizes the year the United States declared its independence.

For almost 4,000 years, the tallest structure in the world was the Great Pyramid of Giza. It remains inspirational as the only one of the original Seven Wonders of the Ancient World that is still relatively intact. I came within a heartbeat of death upon the great complex and still tremble to recall that forbidden midnight exploit. I recall my adventures in the pyramid elsewhere in this book.

India's plethora of intricately carved, white marble Jain temples, Red Forts and Pink Palaces are almost equally enticing and exhausting. I camped in tents, alongside rivers near some of India's 640,000 villages and lodged in dream-like maharajah estates-turned-into-hotels. One of them, the Grand Palace Hotel in Udaipur (Taj Lake Palace) built in the mid-1740s as a royal summer retreat, was converted into a luxurious heritage hotel that truly seems to float like a jewel in the middle of Lake

Pichola. I was most astonished in Chhatarpur, in Madhya Pradesh state, visiting Khajuraho, a group of Hindu and Jain teaching temples that once spread over twenty square kilometres, each one highly decorated with religious and erotic scenes.

Angkor Wat is a magnificent, tree-wrapped temple complex in Cambodia that is renowned for its jaw-dropping architecture. Touted as the largest religious monument in the world, *Angkor Wat* was built by the Khmer King Suryavaram II in the early twelfth century CE. Having served both Hindus and Buddhists, Cambodia's foremost tourist attraction is astounding, but then so is another of the world's seven wonders, *Borobudur,* the incomparable Buddhist temple-mountain in Central Java, dating from the eighth century, as well as *Prambanan,* a nearby ninth-century Hindu temple. We climbed *Borobudur,* shaped like a stepped pyramid, ascending through her three symbolic levels: the Realm of Desire, the Realm of Forms, and the uppermost Realm of Formlessness. We sat among her five hundred meditating Buddhas as we gazed peacefully upon the landscape below and had some of the 3,000 bas-relief sculptures depicting the life of Buddha interpreted for us by a scholarly guide. My twenty-year-old son had his picture taken repeatedly with giggling, Indonesian teenaged girls who were thrilled to be photographed with a handsome exotic foreigner.

Postcard fame does not always account for personal reverberations. Having watched the sun rise on the purity of the *Taj Mahal* and heard the tragic stories associated with it, I feel equally privileged to have circumambulated the *Dhamekha Stupa,* or deer park, in Samath, near the confluence of the Ganges and Varuna rivers, in Uttar Pradesh, where Gautama Buddha first preached the Dharma.

In northern Africa, history came alive for me when I explored the sprawling archaeological remains of Carthage on the coast of Tunisia, only fifteen kilometres from the present capital, Tunis. From here, the Carthaginian general and statesman, Hannibal, once plotted his audacious attack on Rome by leading an army, which included elephants, through the Alps. He never did take Rome and died in Turkey around 183 BCE. The legendary city of Carthage evolved from a Phoenician colony into an empire that dominated the western Mediterranean during the first millennium BCE.

When I visited, the rubble of Carthage touched my soul. The once-magnificent city-state is now a sobering place without any spectacular, man-made ruins. After defeating Carthage in the three Punic Wars (264–146 BCE), the Romans burned the city; they then ploughed the land and sowed it with salt (as they did in Jerusalem in 70 CE) to instill fear, to enact revenge, and so that no crops would ever grow again.

Still magnificent as one of the oldest places of worship in the Islamic world, the nearby Great Mosque of Kairouan has served as the model for all later mosques in the Maghreb. Containing a hypostyle prayer hall, a large marble paved courtyard and a massive square minaret, it is one of the most impressive and largest—yet somehow still unassuming—religious monuments in northern Africa.

The Bardo National Museum in Tunisia is perhaps the second most important museum in Africa, after the Egyptian Museum, affording glimpses of the Blue Koran of Kairouan, a late ninth or early tenth-century manuscript in Kufic calligraphy, likely created in Spain. With its gold lettering on indigo-dyed parchment, this is easily one of the most inspiring works of Islamic calligraphy.

Unfortunately, the Bardo Museum is much less-visited in recent years. Mediterranean tourism to Tunis has sputtered after terrorists stormed the museum on March 18, 2015, killing twenty-two people and injuring another fifty.

The Late Latin (the form of Latin in use between the third and the sixth century CE) term, *Mediterraneum mare,* is a descriptive name owing to its geographical position between northern Africa and southern Europe. Mediterranean derives from *medius* "middle" + *terra* "land, earth" and reads as: Sea in the Middle of the Earth. Until I attended a conference in Tunis, I hadn't realized that the distance from Tunis to Marsala, in Sicily, is only 141 nautical miles (or 162 miles) which is about a half-day's sail, making Tunisia the closest point in North Africa to Europe, other than the distance from Morocco to Gibraltar.

I also had no idea that Tunisia was one of the top olive producing countries in the world, following only Spain, Italy, and Morocco, among others. When, on occasion, the harvest failed in Italy or Spain, Tunisian olives—from some 82 million trees—were exported to fill the gap, with its olive oil often fraudulently labeled as European.

Nearer to Carthage than Tunis, I was inspired by *Sidi Bou Sa'id*, an artists' town that grew around a twelfth-century Sufi *saint et savant*. On a steep cliff with stunning views, it is arguably to Tunisia what Santorini is to Greece, a mecca for photographers because its buildings are painted in deep blues and pure whites. In Islamic countries—as well as in Israeli neighbourhoods inhabited by Jews from Arab lands—many structures, particularly homes, are painted blue, as protection against the evil eye. The entire house does not need to be painted blue, just the doors and shutters, as points of entry are sufficient to ward off danger.

According to folk wisdom, blue is chosen for two reasons: first, it is the colour of the sky and therefore suggests heaven's watchful eye; and, second, it is the colour of the ocean: fish live in the ocean and fish were not drowned during the worst destruction the world has ever known, the flood in the time of Noah. Just the opposite, they thrived. Also, fishes' eyes are always open and therefore a symbol of being ever-watchful against danger. Hence, blue is a protective colour used to evoke a sense of hope and heavenly paradise.

Colour symbolism is important in all traditions. In Islam, for example, green is a symbol of prophecy and nature. Especially for a civilization dwelling in arid, desert conditions, green was a colour associated with vibrant plant life. It is used for the bindings of the Koran and in the silken covers of the graves of Sufi saints. Green and gold are also considered the colours of paradise: When finally reaching paradise in the afterlife, the Koran states, "ornaments shall be given to them therein of bracelets of gold, and they shall wear green robes of fine silk and thick silk brocade interwoven with gold (18:31)" and they will be "Reclining on green cushions set on beautiful carpets (55:76)." White signifies purity and peace. Islamic tradition ascribes white and green as colours that the Prophet Muhammad wore.

MYSTICISM ABOUNDS

Stonehenge, with its origins and purpose shrouded in prehistoric mystery, is a five-thousand-year-old ring of great standing stones, some still capped, within a surrounding earthworks bank-and-ditch circle. Even if one somehow came upon this place with no advance knowledge, they would instinctually appreciate why it has become the object of much speculation in archaeology, history and esoteric studies, attracting all manner of theories. Modern Druidic rites for equinoxes and solstices are still enacted there.

I, too, stood among its ruins—the hood of my sweatshirt encasing my head like a monk's cowl—as a sudden wind began to blow over the hillside, wove itself among the megaliths and caressed my serenely expectant presence. It blew for five minutes during which I was transported into imagined ancient ceremonies. The spectral chanting gradually faded with the afternoon sun, seemingly upon the call of a large resident raven.

In the Americas, I've visited the Mother Church of Christian Science in Boston and heard Christmas Mass at the Cathedral of St. Patrick in New York, but more conspicuously I sat in the presence of dervishes as they whirled in an elegant expression of *dhikr,* or *zikur,* Remembrance of God, in New York's Cathedral of St. John the Divine. As honoured guests of Sheikh Muzaffar, among his Mevlevi Turkish Sufis from Konya, we shared sweet dates, drank bitter coffee and smoked freely flung cigarettes. The Mevlevi Order was founded by the followers of Rumi, the thirteenth-century Persian mystical poet, Islamic jurist and theologian. It was among them that I learned the true meaning of "I will be your servant and you will be my slave."

Conversely, while camped in the woods near New Lebanon, N.Y., under the guidance of the Sufi master, Pir Vilayat Inayat Khan, I once participated in a week-long silent retreat with the humble yet insightful psychic. When I asked his advice as to my path, he offered words of wisdom but I felt as if he saw too much. I squirmed with sudden embarrassment, but it was futile trying to hide from his inner gaze.

In Fidel Castro's Old Havana, I found nothing unusual in the Catholic liturgy when I celebrated Sunday Mass in Spanish at the once-forbidden Cathedral of the Virgin Mary of the Immaculate Conception. The opposite was true when communicating, via translators, with *Santería* priests in both bustling Havana and in sedate Trinidad, a designated World Heritage site.

Santería is the term for a complex system of Afro-Cuban Orisha beliefs that merge aspects of folk religions brought to the Americas by Yoruba slaves with those of Christianity and Indigenous Caribbean traditions. From the early sixteenth century, slaves covertly melded their customs with aspects of Roman Catholicism to perpetuate a trance and divination system (for communicating with their ancestors and deities), animal sacrifice and sacred drumming and dances. I purchased brightly ornamented Ancestor Sticks—prepared as part of *Egun* (ancestral spirits) worship—in exchange for offered blessings and fortune telling from shamanic *Santería* women with an *aumba*. The *aumba* is also known as *opa Egun* (ancestor staff) or *igi Egun* (ancestor stick or branch). It is a staff which is used to call the Egun forth as well as to banish negativity. The style of the *aumba* varies greatly due to many extenuating circumstances surrounding its receipt. In some *Odu* (a reading carried out with small shells) it is required that the *aumba* (the divining tray) is made of a particular wood and that it is to be a particular height. There are also *Odu* which require specific carvings on the *aumba*, such as a two-faced head. As an homage to Nigerian Egungun masquerade, the *aumba* is often decorated with ribbons, strips of cloth and fabric. Mine also includes feathers.

Some landscapes have the capacity to evoke a surprising sense of transparency. That is what I experienced in the verdant valleys, tobacco fields and sculpted mountains of Vinales, Western Cuba. There we climbed a hill in the Vinales Valley to enter the dark mouth of the *Cueva del Indio* (Indian Caves) where we were guided through dark caverns and then boated down a subterranean river into the sudden afternoon sun. I felt like Professor Otto Lidenbrock and his companions in Jules Verne's *A Journey to the Centre of the Earth* when they were swept up into the large volcanic chimney of Mount Stromboli and ejected back onto the Earth's surface.

I have experienced this rare, transformative "Vinales" feeling only five other times on my travels. Each instance is now inextricably bound to the others. The sky seemed higher, the world wider, the soul deeper, and life better. The other five instances were visits to:

- the mystical environs of Tsfat (Safed), the highest city in Israel;
- Delphi, built on a slope of Mount Parnassus surrounded by ruined but still noble temples, site of the ancient Oracle, and with a view down a deep green valley that stretches to the just-visible sea;
- the pathless, rice-terraced mountain fields of Bhutan where the workers sang in unison as they harvested in the Buddhist paradise;
- the numinous rocky folds of Kata Tjuta, the Many Headed Valley of the Winds, in Aboriginal Australia;
- the medieval, walled town of St. Paul de Vence, not far from the *recherché* Riviera in France.

Not all voyages, however, are as satisfying or as elating.

On my visit to Chichén Itza in the north of Mexico's Yucatan Peninsula, I found the former spiritual site, and centre of a Mesoamerican trade network, less-than-inviting. The temperature must have been 40° C, the guide was not only bad but also condescending, and the group was made up of tourists from too many countries. My son and I opted to strike out on our own, giving ourselves the fanciful opportunity to perhaps glimpse a jaguar, an anteater or an armadillo, but settling happily instead for marvelous local birds. Best of all, in a self-imposed time warp, as we wandered away from the tourists and monuments towards a jungle encampment, we encountered gentle folk of short stature, with modest temperaments and round, handsome faces. They were descendants of the Mayans, whose smiles were punctuated by the darkest bright eyes I have ever seen.

Chichén Itza has been included as one of the New Seven Wonders of the World, not the least because it boasts an astrological observatory temple named *El Caracol* ("snail", in Spanish, due to a spiral staircase within), the Temple of the Warriors, and Temples of the Jaguar at the Great Ballcourt with its famous Stone Ring and its Cenote Sagrado, or "Sacred Well". This natural, water-filled sinkhole was a site of sacrificial human offerings to Chac, the god of rain and lightning, whom the Mayans believed dwelled within.

In Mexico, I was most taken by the Kukulkan Pyramid, also known as El Templo or El Castillo. Dedicated to the Mayan feathered serpent deity, Kukulkan, similar to the Aztec god Quetzalcoatl, it is a limestone step-pyramid that dominates the centre of Chichén Itza. It demonstrates the accuracy and significance of Mayan astronomy as well as the heavy influence of the Toltecs who invaded around 1000 CE and precipitated a merger of the two cultural traditions. The temple has 365 steps, one for each day of the year. Each of the temple's four sides has 91 steps, making the very uppermost step on the top platform the 365th step.

I wanted to climb its many steps, wrap myself in its ruins and sit at its temple-top in contemplation of all that transpired below. The pyramid, however, had been closed to climbing a few years earlier because of erosion caused by millions of tourists, graffiti scribbled on the timeworn walls, and the injuries suffered by some visitors, including one who fell to her death.

I reconciled not being permitted to make the risky climb by recalling a short Sufi story called *Climbing the Great Pyramid*. Once upon a time the satirical Sufi, Nasrudin (1208–1284), was seen sitting among the branches of a tree. He was sniffing the blossoms and sunning himself. A traveller asked him what he was doing up the tree. "Climbing the Great Pyramid," he said. The traveller was perplexed.

"You're nowhere near a pyramid. And there are four ways up a pyramid: one by each face. That is a tree!"

"Yes!" said the Mulla. "But it's much more fun like this, don't you think? Birds, blossoms, zephyrs, sunshine. I don't think I could have done better."

Tikal, in nearby Guatemala, boasts Temple IV, the tallest pre-Columbian structure in the Americas, and Tikal National Park covers an area of 576 square kilometres—but I regret I have yet to visit. It is the only locale mentioned in this essay that I have not seen. I've been told it affords a deeper experience of pre-Mayan civilizations than touristy and much-smaller Chichén Itza.

Europe, of course, boasts a plethora of superb architectural gems that can inform and lift the human spirit. Among them, we paid our respects to Saint Peter's Basilica in Rome with its domes, painted ceilings, hidden treasures, and gracefully twisted bronze baldachin over the high altar; thousand-year-old Westminster Abbey in London, site of coronations and royal weddings, burials and bells, cloisters and the nation's memory; and the medieval Catholic cathedral of Notre-Dame de Paris (Our Lady of Paris), with its magnificent stained glass rose windows, flying buttresses and vigilant rooftop gargoyles.

In Spain, I visited the Cathedral of Saint Mary of the See (*Sancta Sedes* in Latin, or the Holy Chair), better known as Seville Cathedral, which is the largest Gothic cathedral and the third-largest church in the world. After its completion in the early sixteenth century, the Seville Cathedral supplanted Hagia Sophia in Istanbul as the largest cathedral in the world, a title the Byzantine church had held for nearly a thousand years.

According to local oral tradition, members of the cathedral chapter said: "*Hagamos una Iglesia tan hermosa y tan grandiosa que los que la vieren labrada nos tengan por locos*" ("Let us build a church so beautiful and so grand that those who see it finished will think we are mad"). The Seville cathedral is also popular as the alleged burial site of Christopher Columbus, even though Santo Domingo in the Dominican Republic also claims to be his final resting place.

Sagrada Familia, Antoni Gaudi's chimerical temple basilica in Barcelona, is world-renowned for its intricately carved, tree-like columns that support the soaring ceilings. Work began in 1882 on what is considered the city's greatest building; it is now entering its final phase of construction. When completed, this will be the tallest religious structure in Europe. Walking through the grand building filled with layers of symbolism and bathed in waves of ethereal colour that immerses one in a transcendent dreamscape, cares of the outside world soon drop away, and the visitor becomes transported into the realm of the sacred.

Set within the stunning, multi-peaked mountain of Montserrat, about an hour's drive north-west from Barcelona, is the noble Benedictine retreat of Santa Maria de Montserrat. Taking care to arrive before the crowds expected for Sunday's Catholic Mass, my son, Avi, and I ascended the altar to view the Black Madonna, lit candles in contemplation caves, and, on adjoining cliffs, saw the outline of collapsed hovels and nearly unreachable caves that were the abandoned abodes of reclusive hermit monks.

Montserrat literally means "saw (serrated, like the teeth on a saw) mountain" in Catalan. The extended mountain—composed of a striking pink conglomerate, a form of sedimentary rock—forms a spectacular landmark. It is easy to envisage the landscape being the subject of prehistoric mythopoetic imaginings and, before Christ, the Romans built a temple dedicated to Venus at Montserrat. Tour guides do little to dispel the assertion that the monastery contains the Holy Grail from Arthurian legend. Before descending the holy mountain, we sat at a vantage point above the square as it filled with devotees, smoked an illegally procured joint and were enraptured by the continuous tolling of huge, centuries-old abbey bells.

In Andalusia—in southern Spain where the architecture had been influenced by centuries of Islamic Moorish presence—we spent a Sabbath weekend visiting the magnificent palace fortress of Alhambra in Granada (sometimes described as the Eighth Wonder of the World). A two-hour's drive away is the site of another outstanding religious edifice: the mosque-now-cathedral of Córdoba. Filled with a vast assembly of arches, pillars and hovering ceilings, it is one of the most significant architectural accomplishments of the past two millennia.

In St. Petersburg, I was awed by two magnificent multi-onion-domed Russian Orthodox churches: Saint Isaac's Cathedral, where we also attended Sunday services during which one remains standing the entire time, and the Church of the Saviour on Spilled Blood, a fantasy structure almost completely covered in mosaic tiles depicting gospel narratives. One must really listen to Russian Orthodox chants to understand the power of these services. Many are available online.

St. Basil's Cathedral, in Moscow's Red Square, just outside the Kremlin, was commissioned by Ivan the Terrible in the mid-sixteenth century. With its series of colourful domes and redbrick towers, St. Basil's has been aptly described as a "riot of colour and shapes." Its interior, just as densely decorated, caused the French diplomat Marquis de Custine to wonder at "the men who go to worship God in this box of confectionery work." I, however, was moved by the unpretentious sincerity of the service. I was also enamoured with Orthodox worship, characterized by harmonious chanting, generous clouds of fragrant incense and honeyed candles in humble settings.

Much has been written about the graceful, pillared ruins of the Parthenon in Athens and other temples scattered throughout Greece. Notably, these include the ruins of Corinth, the ancient city roughly halfway between Athens and Sparta on the narrow stretch of land that joins the Peloponnese to the mainland. Its inhabitants were the inspiration for Paul's letters to the Corinthians (the books 1 and 2 Corinthians in the Bible).

In Epidaurus, I paid homage to the Healing Temple sacred to Asclepius, the Grecian God of Medicine, but was later disheartened by the state of the Elysian Fields, site of The Eleusinian Mysteries—the most famous of the secret religious rites of ancient Greece—where initiations were held every year for the cult of Demeter and Persephone. Perhaps it was undergoing restoration, for when I visited it was a ruin within a ruin on a back street surrounded by a chain-link fence.

I drove to Olympia (not to be confused with Mount Olympus in central Greece) in the Peloponnese, the site of the original Olympic Games. Some old race tracks still exist and so, reasoning that this was the closest that I was ever going to get to the Olympics, I ran a makeshift solitary dash—and won. These Hellenic journeys were all in autumn, well past the summer tourist season, so there was no one else around.

Closer to home, I have been enthralled by a few old-growth forests including the aptly-named Cathedral Grove, a 157-hectare stand of Douglas fir trees in MacMillan Provincial Park, in central Vancouver Island.

More Grounds For Worship

In the progression of worship, it was first the tree or mountain that was itself recognized as a deity, then they became the abodes of the deity, until the deity evolved into a non-corporeal spirit and moved into a heavenly penthouse in the remote regions of infinite space. Great trees, mountains and rocks, however, continue to evoke the supernatural.

Mythical mountains have been identified in traditional societies across the world. These include Mount Meru, navel of the world for Hindus, Buddhists and Jain, and considered the centre of all the physical, metaphysical and spiritual universes; the very real Mount Kailas in Tibet, considered holy to four religions—Hindus, Jains, Tibetan Buddhists and the native Bon in Tibet; Mount Olympus, home of the gods, in Greece; the Kunlun Mountains protecting the western edge of Shangri-La and a Taoist paradise; Mount Ararat—the traditional landing place of Noah's ark—now in eastern Turkey but traditionally identified with Armenia ("the people of Ararat"); and the Jade Mountain of Chinese folklore. There are hundreds more.

A further stage of religious development is that the numen has no specific, limiting address in either celestial or terrestrial realms but is now perceived as being omnipresent, omniscient and omnipotent. For animists, Nature *is* their temple. This is in contrast to others who may appreciate nature for its beauty, its status as a homeland, or its utilitarian uses in procuring food or extracting mineral wealth, but who construct altars, shrines and edifices *upon* the land.

Some high spots were built on mountains and others were the mountains themselves. Among these were the sundry Temples of the Sun, the Moon, the Earth and Heaven in China where I also visited the Forbidden City, the Summer Palace with its Imperial Gardens, climbed the gravity-laden Great Wall and spent several days in Suzhou—an important 2,500-year-old city known for its gardens, canals, stone bridges, arts and economy that has been called the "Venice of the East". Much better known to me, and where I lived for six years, is the golden-domed Temple Mount in Jerusalem.

The effects on pilgrims visiting *Yerushalayim* can be so profound that psychiatrists have named it the "Jerusalem syndrome" after mental phenomena involving religiously-themed obsessive ideas or delusions. Not to be confused with the Stockholm syndrome, these pertain to psychotic experiences triggered by a visit to the city. Some individuals come to believe they are a prophet with miraculous powers, the Messiah or the second coming of Jesus. I have known three people who developed such conditions and I've seen others in the streets. Not all survive. This behaviour has also been observed in Mecca and Rome.

On many occasions I have visited the archaeological and religious sites of Jerusalem and found moments of inspiration. One such occasion was when my father accompanied me to the Mount of Olives. As we walked among its ancient graves, a whirlwind swept the hillside and blew his white hair into a halo around his experienced head. I didn't want to say anything at first but then I dared to tell him that he looked like a prophet who had returned to walk among his people. The landscape can do things like that to you, especially in places like *Yerushalayim*.

I am familiar with the history of the Canaanites, Babylonians, Assyrians, Egyptians, Greeks, Romans, Persians, Crusaders, Ottomans and many others who wanted to control the narrow land bridge—known today as Israel—that joins Europe, Asia and Africa. After a two-thousand-year exile, Jewish immigrants from over 120 countries have returned to Zion. For Jews, there are many significant spiritual sites in Israel and the surrounding environs. I will, however, relate the story of only one. It was the site of the Holy Temple.

Once, with a semi-forbidden, small group, I walked seven times around the gold-plated Dome of the Rock at the centre of the Al-Aqsa Mosque compound in the Old City of Jerusalem and then descended to witness the rocky outcropping within. It is known as the *Ehven ha'Shtiyah*, the Foundation Stone or Noble Rock. This is the traditional site from where God created the world as well as Adam, the first human. It was also identified with Mount Moriah, where Abraham nearly sacrificed Isaac, and where, according to rabbinic midrash, Jacob had his dream about the angel-filled ladder reaching to heaven. It also became the centre of the Jewish world and the location upon which the *Beit Ha'Mikdash*, the Holy Temples, were built before being destroyed first by the Babylonians in 586 BCE and then by the Romans in 70 CE. Jesus, in his time, walked these grounds and, in Islamic lore, it is the focal point for Mohammed's Night Journey astride *Buraq*, the heavenly winged steed assigned to transport prophets. Others have professed this is also where the tablets of the Ten Commandments were hidden. Sacred sites attract their many stories.

If there is any other city that resonates almost as deeply with me as Jerusalem, it would have to be Venice, the sinking city of Temporal Enchantments, with its bridges and gondolas; with its cafes, galleries and workshops; carnivals, concerts and masquerades; its churches, winged-Venetian lion pillars, plazas, charming hotels and distinctive neighbourhoods; its Gothic palazzos built on the sea and the labyrinthian canals that make getting lost an art, and, which then make being found, finally, the sum of a worthy adventure.

Significantly, for me, is that Venezia is also the city of Marco Polo, who was reputedly born and grew up here (Croatia also claims him as a native son). It is also his final resting place. As I stood in front of his ancestral home, I knew him as the Master of Travellers, the one who dared. Early in my adult life I had vowed that I, too, would follow his resolve and affirm the struggle leading to wonder, discovery, knowledge and the sharing of my possessions and my mind. The airport in Venice, portal to the world, is fittingly named for him. He inspired a continent to look far and to travel long.

COLDER REALMS OF WONDER

Whereas Venice is built on land borrowed from the sea, the Arctic, for the most part, *is* the sea. The Arctic is a frozen ocean surrounded by territory of eight northern nations.

The Arctic in the north and Antarctica in the south have deep personal significance as high points in my explorations. In addition, I was blessed to have transformative polar experiences in both places that can be compared to the major epiphanies which I experienced in the Alexandrian catacombs and in the dark, carved chambers beneath the Great Pyramid.

In the Arctic I heard Inuit throat singers, met their elders, been invited into their homes, hugged them tight and pinned to my coat a carved bone image of a spirit-possessed shaman beating his otherworldly drum. I have worn Greenland clothing woven from *qiviut* (the downy underwool of the muskox) and have been mesmerized by sun dogs (a sun dog, or ice bow, is created by sunlight reflecting off the ice particles in the atmosphere, similar to a rainbow).

Another time and almost 20,000 kilometres apart, sitting in the Antarctic peninsula among penguins, beneath a deep blue sky on a low hill overlooking a truly azure sea, I again felt the shackles of society—of all cultures and civilizations—fall away. These cultures and civilizations tried to argue themselves back into my favour by claiming significant discoveries, conveniences and advances in science; they spoke of Paris Opera houses, scholarship, art and architecture; they debated for the virtues of courts, ethics, and social services, and tempted me with other tantalizing persuasions.

But I was calm, thankful and filled with the peace that only comes from an unknowing rebirth into a nascent cosmos. Everything was *just as it was*: no words, no labels, instructions or demands.

I smiled at the penguin who approached me—perhaps he intuited my state of mind—and felt a thoroughly fulfilling peace for perhaps only the third time in my life.

That night I wrote to a friend.

Since I was young, I always wanted to travel and experience the entire world firsthand. I remember how exhilarating it was to cross the equator for the first time. Gradually, but then wholeheartedly, I appreciated geography as an extension of my body, my psyche. Everywhere I travelled in the outer world opened up corresponding dimensions in the inner realms.

Travelling to the poles was a gradual process of first going on exploratory trips to both the Arctic and Antarctic. I then focused on the essence of north and south. When I travelled to the North Pole, I kept it a secret from most people. I hardly told myself. It was too special, too rare. It wasn't long after my return, however, that I was drawn to its balancing counterpart in the South. These travels were not burdened by any concerns or agendas. It was more of an intuitive imperative, a pilgrimage to the ends of the Earth so that I might know both the planet and myself better.

We are part of a cosmic continuum that permeates the uni-

Haida Gwaii, 2022. Photo by Avi Wosk

verse. Or, as the founder of the *Whole Earth Catalog*, Stuart Brand, quipped: "It's interesting to think that outer space begins at your feet."

Each step we take creates echoes in the landscape as well as the soul. Our planet is only the local manifestation of universal principles. It offers a frame of reference and guides us to recognize that we are all part of an extended, interconnected web of wonders and field of dreams. As is the way with dreams, some are confusing while others become nightmares. All we can strive to do is to wake up; dream on, dream better.

DEATH AND OTHER PURSUITS

Cemeteries and Mausoleums

By the sweat of frustration you shall eat bread until you return to the ground, because out of it you were taken; for dust you are and to dust you shall return. — Genesis 3:19

Labour not after riches first and think that you will enjoy them afterwards. One who neglects the present moment throws away all that he has. It is like a warrior wounded by an arrow passing through his heart: he didn't know that it was coming. So shall your life be taken away before you know that you have it. — Egyptian Book of the Dead

After visiting St. Peter's Square and the Vatican library, craning my neck to absorb Michelangelo's Sistine Chapel ceiling, I descended to the crypt below the *Baldacchino di San Pietro*. There, perhaps, a grander journey begins. There can be no greater "act of geography" than being buried, than consigning our bodies, our ashes, our remains, to the Earth.

The final resting place for some is the beginning of imagination for others.

We can easily imagine other lives and loves, struggles and accomplishments; we take instruction from their mistakes and inspiration from their victories. Some lived long; others, hardly at all. We are born of the Earth and return to its lingering embrace. Some are mourned and buried; others are unknown and relinquished to the indifferent elements.

Cemeteries elicit a maelstrom of mixed emotions including intimations of immortality, abandonment to our fate, repentance from past transgressions, resolutions to improve in the future and contemplations on the meaning of life. They are the home of the humbled; we are their custodians, respectfully engaged in perpetual care.

In my role as clergy I've assisted with the burial of too many fine people: recited prayers between death and burial; and arranged for the body to be prepared by the *Hevra Kadisha*, the Holy Society, who take care of *tahara* and *takhrikhim,* washing the body and garbing it in pure white shrouds. I've consoled family and friends; prepared and delivered eulogies through broken hearts and trembling lips; accompanied bodies on their final journeys in the back of long black hearses; lowered caskets into deeply dug graves and shovelled soil until the casket was respectfully covered.

After the burial we asked forgiveness from the dead in case we might have offended them during these last rites.

There are many kinds of burial, many ways to return to the Earth. I have visited pyramids of mummified pharaohs; paid respects to the honoured interment of royalty and priests, writers, scientists, heroes and politicians under the hallowed stone floors of Westminster Abbey; smoked ganga, the "holy herb or wisdom weed" at Nine Mile, the Jamaican mountain mausoleum of the reggae man Bob Marley; and gone on pilgrimages to cemeteries populated with fascinating headstones, grave markers, monuments and mausoleums.

Some of the noteworthy cemeteries include *Cimitero Monumentale* in Milan, *La Recoleta* in Buenos Aires and Mount Auburn in Boston, founded in 1831 and now a National Historic Landmark. *La Recoleta*, in particular, is one of the world's most extraordinary graveyards with over 6,400 grandiose mausoleums resembling Gothic chapels, Greek temples, fairy tale grottoes and elegant little houses for, among so many others, Eva Perón (affectionately known as Evita).

I've also paid homage at Inuit and Danish cemeteries in Greenland (they are frozen for much of the year which makes for difficult grave digging). Over the centuries and depending on conditions, many Inuit, as well as explorers, must have been buried in the ice, beneath the frigid waters, or in makeshift land-based cemeteries. The Inuit generally buried their dead under cairns (structures of piled stones) on the surface of the land or ice.

Today, funerals are conducted according to religious beliefs, as many Inuit have converted to Christianity. On Beechey Island, located in the Canadian Arctic Archipelago of Nunavut, we paid our respects at a solitary site that held the graves of three sailors from the Franklin Expedition in search of the Northwest Passage. Although they were buried in 1846, the constantly freezing temperatures preserved the bodies. The intense cold had turned them into mummies; these had intact soft tissue that when carefully thawed could be analysed.

There are two kinds of mummies: first, the dead body of a human being or animal ceremoniously preserved by mummification. The ancient Egyptian process included removal of the internal organs, treatment with natron and resin, and then wrapping the body in bandages or some similar method of embalming. Other cultures that mummified their ancestors included Australian aboriginals, Aztec and Inca, some Africans, Indigenous Europeans and some age-old Chinese communities, among others. The second kind is a dead body preserved by its natural environment.

In Cairo, we drove through the unique *el-Arafa* necropolis, known in English as the City of the Dead. The oldest parts of the necropolis were established more than 700 years ago. Cairo is so overcrowded today that tens of thousands of its citizens live among the million tombs. Some move there out of necessity but there are other reasons to dwell among the dead: many believe that living beside the shrines of the deceased, predominantly saints and scholars, is a blessing that will bring divine reward, while others wish to be close to their ancestors.

I've also seen rooms of neatly stacked monks' bones in the catacombs beneath Rome and in the Greek Orthodox monastery of Saint Catherine's at the foot of Mt. Sinai, the world's oldest, continuously inhabited Christian monastery. I've also visited *Kivrei HaSanhedrin*, a first century underground complex of sixty-three rock-cut tombs of the Sanhedrin located in northern Jerusalem.

Concealed beneath the seaside city of Alexandria are the catacombs of *Kom el Shoqafa*, the most important Greco-Roman necropolis in Egypt and which is one of the Seven Wonders of the Middle Ages.

These catacombs were cut into three levels of bedrock beneath the old city but the third level is now submerged under water. These levels consist of catacombs, ceremonial and funeral banquet rooms, decorated stone sarcophagi, mosaics and paintings, bas relief and full dimensional sculptures, arches, pillars and small temples, all set among a mixture of Egyptian, Greek and Roman architecture.

As we descended the rotunda ever deeper down the large, stone-cut spiral staircase and into the catacombs, I was drawn to experience those age-old final resting places for myself. As our guide and group moved ahead into the next chamber, I tarried behind and disappeared down unknown passageways.

All that remained was a dim light and the kind of muffled silence that dwells among stone walls dug deep in the Earth: everything was absorbed, even the sound of one's breath and, after a few moments, the sound of thought itself.

I was somewhat concerned that I would not be able to find the tour again and I would remain lost among the dead, but the call was strong and opportunity fleeting, so I dared to abandon myself to an experiment among the long-deceased denizens, readers of the Book of the Dead.

I chose a singular catacomb grave, one of many stone cavities carved two or three high into the rock walls. It had been occupied for 1,600 years but was empty now and awaited its date with this visitor from the future.

I crawled in, headfirst and on my back, to a space that was smaller than it seemed. At first it felt somewhat frightening and claustrophobic but after slowing my mind and calming my respiration, I began to feel a boundless peace.

There, in the care of Osiris—the Egyptian deity, usually identified as the god of the afterlife, the underworld, and the dead, but more appropriately as the god of transition, resurrection and regeneration—the anxieties and responsibilities of my earthly life fell away.

At first they disappeared one by one but then in thematic purges: Not having to worry about finances, jobs and business, paying bills, making appointments, dressing up, minding manners, caring for health, family matters, always learning and enslaved by curiosity, diet as to what to eat, how much, when, and what not to ingest ever, how to speak, what to say, what not to say, the drama of sexuality, using time wisely and not wasting a moment, seeking directions, making war and professing peace, dealing with emotions, the weather, the home, creativity, desire for goods and power, rights and wrongs, courts and judgments, dealing with countless daily seductions and so many more thousands of concerns that plague the living.

A series of great weights were lifted from my now semi-comatose body resting motionless in the grave.

The relief afforded by each abandonment took me closer to childhood, then to being an infant, then to floating in the womb, and finally to a time of infinite possibilities before my progenitors knew one another, before and after Creation, into the mysteries beyond. Zen teaching proposes an impossible question: "What did your original face look like before you were born?" Now I knew. Meta-silence had cast its spell: no face, no matter.

One of my teachers, Zalman Schachter-Shalomi, used to tell us that you don't have to wait until you're dead to die; that one can be involved in a succession of deaths and rebirths, that there is non-mortal death and resurrection while still alive. Although it felt like I had been embedded in a fragment of eternity, ten minutes later I extricated myself from the grave, reluctantly became reoriented to my surroundings and went off in search of companions.

Worry and want would invade me once again but at least I would be among friends.

Since the Jews would not bury their dead inside the city walls, Jerusalem is surrounded by tombs. To the east of the city is Mount Scopus, *Har Ha'Tsofim,* translated as "Mount of the Spectators" or "Lookout Mountain," one of the few places from which both the Dead Sea to the east and the Dome of the Rock to the west can be seen. The British Military Cemetery on Mount Scopus, also known as the Jerusalem War Cemetery, houses the graves of more than 2,500 fallen Commonwealth soldiers who battled the Ottoman Empire during the First World War in order to conquer the city.

On an adjacent hill is the Jewish cemetery on *Har Ha'Zaitim,* the Mount of Olives. Including the Silwan necropolis, it is the most ancient and important cemetery in Jerusalem. The Silwan necropolis is assumed to have been used by the highest-ranking officials residing in Jerusalem. Situated on the rocky eastern slope of the Kidron Valley facing the oldest part of Jerusalem, its tombs were cut between the ninth and seventh centuries BCE. The Arab village of Silwan was later built on top of it.

Burial on the Mount of Olives started some 3,000 years ago in the First Temple Period and continues to this day. The cemetery contains about 70,000 tombs from various periods including those of prominent figures in Jewish history. Some of the tombs on *Har Ha'Zaitim* are located in the Kidron Valley where, according to tradition, the Messiah—with pure olive oil dripping from his anointed head and long beard—is to appear to raise the dead, judge humankind and enter the Temple on Mount Moriah. Some prefer to be buried there so they will be able to accompany the Messenger of Redemption and be among the first to witness peace in the fulfillment of history.

I have visited other Jewish cemeteries around the world including those in Frankfurt am Main, Gibraltar and Prague, which is home to the largest Jewish cemetery in Europe. In Hebrew, a cemetery is variously termed as *beit kevarot* ("place of the sepulchres"; Nehemia 2:3, Sanh. 6:5); *beit olam* ("house of eternity"; see Ecclesiastes 12:5) or its Aramaic form *beit almin* (Ecclesiastes R. 10:9, Targ. Isa. 40:11); *beit mo'ed le-khol hai* ("the house appointed for all living"; Job 30:23); or euphemistically *beit hayyim* ("house of the living").

In Prague—walking among the crowded, tumbled stones—in some areas the dead were often buried in layers. During the more than three centuries in which it was in active use, the cemetery continually struggled with its lack of space. Piety and respect for the deceased ancestors does not allow the Jews to abolish old graves. Only occasionally was the Jewish Community allowed to purchase grounds to expand the cemetery. Often, it had to gain space in other ways: if needed, a new layer of soil was heaped up on the available area.

For this reason, in the Prague cemetery there are places where as many as twelve layers now exist. Thanks to this solution, the older graves themselves remained intact. However, as new levels were added it was necessary either to lay over the gravestones associated with the older (and lower) graves to protect them, or else to elevate the stones to the new, higher surface.

This explains the dense forest of gravestones that one sees today; many of them commemorate an individual who is buried several layers further down. This also explains why the surface of the cemetery is raised several meters higher than the surrounding streets; retaining walls are required to hold the soil and the graves in place.

Not far away is the Old New Synagogue, the *Altneuschul*, situated in Josefov, the old Jewish Quarter in Prague. It is Europe's oldest active synagogue and one of the city's first Gothic buildings. According to legend, angels brought stones from King Solomon's Temple to build the synagogue: those same angels still protect it. Another folktale connects the shul to the Golem, a humanoid creature fashioned from clay and animated with the mystic arts in the sixteenth century by Rabbi Yehuda ben Betzalel Loew (1512–1609), better known as the Maharal of Prague (*Moreinu HaRav Loew* [Our Teacher, Rabbi Loew]) to defend the Jews from persecution. The Golem was made dormant and placed in a garret, but it can be awakened again when needed.

Franz Kafka attended this synagogue when he lived in Prague and his bar mitzvah was held there.

War graves and monuments are many: every city has them, every nation accommodates its victims. Some nations have also been the aggressors, convicted of atrocious crimes. I've visited war-torn countries where everyone lost a family member in battle or a war crime, and if they didn't they knew someone who did. I have also stood before Eternal Flames and Graves of the Unknown Soldier in a number of countries, including Russia, where approximately ten million civilians and another ten million soldiers were killed during the Second World War. Among the largest cemeteries dedicated to soldiers who died in war, or veterans who died later and wanted to be interred there, is Arlington National Cemetery across the Potomac River from Washington, D.C., where I visited the Tomb of the Unknowns and the gravesite Memorial to President John F. Kennedy.

We also made a pilgrimage to Hiroshima, the sudden grave of over a hundred thousand people. The bomb was dropped on Hiroshima on August 6, 1945; another one fell on Nagasaki three days later. Within four months of the bombings, the acute effects killed between 70,000 to 146,000 civilians and soldiers in Hiroshima and between 40,000 and 80,000 in Nagasaki. Roughly half of the deaths in each city occurred on the first day; others succumbed to injuries or radiation-related illnesses in the following months and years.

The atomic bomb was originally developed to help defeat the Nazis in Europe but when that theatre was closed, with the surrender of German forces on May 9, 1945, all eyes turned to the Pacific. I had conversations about the dropping of the bomb with American veterans I knew in Boston. While they didn't welcome the high civilian death toll, they were unanimous in declaring that the atomic bombs and the subsequent surrender of the Japanese forces soon after, actually saved about one million lives—the estimated number of Allied and Japanese soldiers and civilians, who would have been killed if the war had dragged on for another couple of years. The Second World War—the most destructive conflict in human history, with an estimated death toll of approximately 60 million, was officially ended but millions more continued to suffer. War *is* hell.

As a belated witness to the worst atrocities ever perpetrated by our disturbed species, I visited Nazi concentration camps, Mauthausen and Auschwitz, two among many in the elaborate German bureaucracy of death. It is widely agreed that more than six million Jews perished during the Holocaust, most of whom were brutally murdered. That was two-thirds of European Jewry. Another five million people were murdered, those who were considered racially or biologically inferior such as the Roma, Germans with physical or mental disabilities, and some of the Slavic peoples (especially Poles and Russians). Additional persecutions were those eliminated for political or ideological reasons or those implicated in what the Nazis considered criminal behaviour, including Jehovah's Witnesses, homosexuals, Communists and others who resisted.

The pre-war worldwide Jewish population has been estimated at eighteen million. Approximately one-and-a-half million Jewish children—about ninety percent of Europe's prewar Jewish population of children—were murdered by the German Nazis and their collaborators; only 100,000 survived. In those days, in the Kingdom of Death among the ashes of Auschwitz where burial was *verboten* and only tortured dust remained, there was hardly a return to the Earth, for it, too, was scorched, bodies branded and burned, graves concealed, the Final Solution almost completed.

And still there are other ways to return to the Earth for there are, unfortunately, a thousand ways to die. I've known too many who died from inadvertent drug overdoses, those who committed suicide when mental or physical pain drove them to desperation, met survivors of the Rwandan genocide and walked the Killing Fields of Cambodia.

We cry "Never Again" and yet there are too many *agains,* and not enough *nevers*; too many other acts of genocide when the earth, not always silent, is forced to accept the violated bodies of her innocent offspring.

In contrast to genocide, where the perpetrators often try to conceal evidence of their atrocities (though they may consider them to be grand accomplishments), humans tend to have an opposite predilection to preserve life and to achieve immortality either in this world or in a world to come. The conundrum results from the paradox of our minds being able to imagine immortality but our bodies not able to sustain it. Death is considered a defeat, a negative phenomenon, and a weakness when compared to the ideal. For these reasons history is filled with fable, religions, philosophy and science that describe the quest for the elixir of eternal life. And not just eternal life but also immortality accompanied by great strength and vibrant health—growing old yet remaining young.

As John Donne (1572–1631) wrote in his posthumously published "Sonnet 10": "Death, be not proud [...] Death, thou shalt die."

The pyramids of the pharaohs are perhaps the most famous of such ventures, with others being the Epic of Gilgamesh, the amrita of India, ambrosia of the Greeks, immortal peaches of China, golden apples of Greece, the alchemists in pursuit of *Lapis Philosophorum,* and particular practices of the Aztecs, Mayans and Incas.

Who could forget a visit to the massive, concealed burial site of Qin Shi Huang, the first Emperor of China in the third century BCE? Located about forty kilometres east of the ancient capital and still partially walled city of Xi'an in central China, this site holds the Terracotta Army, a collection of over 8,000 life-size terracotta sculptures depicting the emperor's armies—including warriors, chariots and horses—as well as non-military officials, acrobats, strongmen and musicians. Their purpose was to protect and serve the emperor in his afterlife.

On a quiet, rainy, summer afternoon, I finally had an opportunity to visit the Tomb of Lenin (1870–1924) in Red Square just outside the Kremlin. Upon seeing his perfectly preserved body, I gasped and was told to keep quiet by a stern Russian uniformed armed guard. I had an opportunity to also view Chairman Mao Tse-tung's preserved body in a mausoleum in Tiananmen Square but demurred. It wasn't just the long line-up. I had reservations about paying respects to Mao (1893–1976) whose policies and actions made him one of the twentieth century's most diabolical mass murderers alongside Stalin and Hitler. Estimates vary widely as to how many were killed or died under his rule—between 40 to 80 million, whether it was through war, starvation, persecution, forced labour or mass executions.

In St. Petersburg, I visited the graves of Russian luminaries including Tchaikovsky and Dostoevsky buried at Aleksander Nevsky Monastery in the Necropolis of Masters of Art where, as I have described elsewhere in this book, I left our private tour behind and planted myself in front of Dostoevsky's sculptural tomb where I engaged in an imaginal conversation with the great writer.

I had a similarly meditative conversation at a nearly inaccessible monastery in the Tibetan mountains about a hundred miles from Lhasa. It was the school of the young Dalai Lama's principal teacher. I approached the master's now-empty low cushioned chair, bowed and asked for his spectral advice. I was told that I was on the right path, to keep focused, to return home and continue to put my affairs, including future initiatives, in order. Abandoning, escaping, or running from life's responsibilities would be counterproductive. Discipline was key to principled production in the present as well as creative accomplishment in the future. Without this dedicated discipline I could not evolve to the next level. Akin to being told to go on a diet or get more exercise, this was not necessarily what I wanted to hear but I knew it was right.

And then there was Varanasi, considered the spiritual capital of India and the holiest of the seven sacred cities. It is a vibrant nexus of exaggerated life, sanctified death and the maelstrom of everything in-between. We took a late afternoon ride in a horse-drawn open carriage through the bustling market followed by a candlelit night ceremony accompanied by waves of Hindu musicians, blaring horns, clanging cymbals and drifting fire flowers on the holy Ganges River, worshipped as the goddess Ganga.

Early the next morning we returned to visit sadhus and fakirs, beggars and charlatans, to view temples and palaces, but mostly to approach riverside ghats to watch—with a mixture of curiosity, strangeness and reverence—the constant cremation of bodies on a maze of open funeral pyres. The ashes were scattered upon the Holy River whose waters are equated with nectar in Indian tradition. Here there is no return to the ground but rather consignment to the flames and waters, another gateway for a peaceful journey to heaven.

There are so many exits on the way out of life. There is no right or wrong way how to remember the deceased or how to handle the corpse: some offer it to the birds, others burn, bury or preserve it through such techniques as mummification and cryogenics. We are born as one "in the image of God," live a short life—characterized by a modicum of beauty, love and learning but mostly by struggle, desire and arrogant illusion—only to return to Thanatos, when all are equal once again.

MOUNTAINS, ROCKS, CAVES AND CAVERNS

I have camped in deserts under black night skies hung with waves of unending stars and on summer glaciers where the sun never sets. When a student in the Holy Land, I visited the walled Greek Orthodox monastery, Santa Katarina (Saint Catherine's), in the remote God-trodden South Sinai where I saw antiquarian scrolls and the rarest of manuscripts (the second-largest collection, after the Vatican Library, in the world), centuries of carefully arranged monks' bones and the alleged site of the Burning Bush from which God encountered Moses. The next morning, I climbed Mount Sinai in the darkness before dawn and reached the wind-swept summit with sunrise.

I have ascended the volcanic Vesuvius—harbinger of doom for Pompeii and Herculaneum and the only active volcano on mainland Europe—and peered over the summit into her still-smoking crater. Small mountains and high hills were also scaled in China, Tibet, Bhutan, the Antarctic, United States, Canada, Greece, the deserts of Jordan and in Israel.

I've been drawn to smooth river rocks and glacier-dropped erratic boulders, smiled as a child at the surprising glint of mica and quartz set in granite, and have been astonished at the $250 million deep-blue Hope Diamond (also known as *Le Bijou du Roi*, "the King's Jewel") along with the Star of Asia sapphire. I have viewed moon rocks and meteorites at the Smithsonian's National Gem and Mineral Collection in the National Museum of Natural History in Washington, D.C.

I also visited the two other most significant natural history museums in the United States: the Field Museum of Natural History in Chicago, and the American Museum of Natural History in New York, one of the world's pre-eminent scientific and cultural institutions. It was there, in 1977, that I saw Margaret Mead walking its corridors with her long wooden staff on her way to a public lecture, which I attended.

I've contemplated Japanese dry landscape rock gardens, including the fifteen perfectly placed stones in Ryoanji Zen Temple in Kyoto; collected stones from exotic locations (such as Easter Island in the South Pacific, Blarney Castle in Ireland, and the Antarctic Peninsula) or just because they were spellbinding; and climbed over mountain ridges as well as large beach boulders. A mysterious Wiccan named Ann once gifted me with a brilliant blue rough lapis lazuli rock, a purported fragment of the elusive Philosopher's Stone of alchemical knowledge and eternal life. On our last day in Nepal, I purchased an expensive character-laden necklace made from coarse coral that reminded me of terrestrial teeth. Mined in the Himalayas, the remnant of prehistory was formed at least fifty million years ago when the great Asiatic landmass was deep beneath the ocean.

As for mountains, I've been introduced to the Himalayas (the highest mountain range in the world), the Andes (the longest) as well as the Alps, the Alaska Range, the Transantarctic Mountains, the Great Dividing Range or Eastern Highlands of Australia, the Great Escarpment of southern Africa and the Rocky Mountains that extend like a spine through much of western North America, from northern British Columbia and Alberta, down to New Mexico. Mount Fuji—perhaps the most iconic of mountains, and considered the most holy height in Japan with Sengen, the Shinto Goddess of Fujiyama, living within—was glimpsed in many guises including her emerging shyly from a veil of kimono cloud.

I was also gratified to visit the island of Santorini with its blue-domed whitewashed churches and picturesque villages that cling to cliffs above the ocean. The Santorinian caldera in the southern Aegean Sea is the site of one of the largest volcanic eruptions in recorded history, which occurred approximately 3,600 years ago. Popular theory claims that the eruption is the source of the legend of Atlantis.

In the same category, but a world away and never permanently populated, is Deception Island, the caldera of an active volcano, in the South Shetland Islands archipelago. With one of the safest harbours in Antarctica, this island was formerly used for sealing and whaling but is now a tourist destination and a base for scientific research.

In Hawaii—geographically defined as a volcanic archipelago in the Central Pacific Ocean—many mountains are accorded sacred status by the Indigenous peoples as well as prime destinations for millions of tourists to the islands. I visited many of these locations including Kauai—the oldest, northernmost, and lushest island in the Hawaiian chain, and site for films and honeymoons, including my own—featuring its spectacular Na Pali Coast, Waimea Canyon and Wailua Falls; the impressively symmetrical Diamond Head—prominently visible from everywhere in Waikiki—where we undertook a steep, one-kilometre hike to the crater's rim in the volcanic cone; as well as Haleakalā, a massive shield volcano that forms over seventy-five percent of Maui.

On the Big Island of Hawaii—the largest and youngest of the islands where the summits of the five volcanoes are revered as sacred mountains—are the active volcanoes of Kilauea and Mauna Loa. Nearby is Mauna Kea, an extinct volcano, which is the highest mountain (13,800 feet / 4,205 metres) in the Pacific Basin. If its enormous underwater mass is included, it would be the tallest mountain in the world.

I am remiss in not yet visiting Peli, the goddess of fire, volcanoes and lightning, of dancing winds and the rhythmic movements of life; she is also considered to be the creator of the Hawaiian Islands. Reputed to live in Halemaʻumaʻu crater, located within the much larger summit caldera of Kilauea, epithets for the goddess include *Pele-honua-mea* ("Pele of the sacred land") and *Ka wahine ʻai honua* ("The earth-eating woman"). Two of my teachers—one an artist with a camera, the other a mystic in a trance—spoke highly of the volcanic mountain and its resident immortal.

A relentless curiosity has motivated me to study, write and lecture about geography of the sacred centre, world trees and cosmic oceans. I have transited contemporary wonders of the world, the Suez and Panama Canals where I was glued to the ship's deck so as not to miss a minute of these extraordinary feats of engineering. I gazed at the immense significance, both historically and geographically, of the Corinth Canal in Greece. I've seen Grand Canyons carved by relentless rivers and shaped by determined winds, and explored Sinai desert weather-worn, high-walled, canyon trails in the wilderness.

Different but equally impressive, both as geographic formation and inspirational landscape, is *Uluru*, the largest monolith in the world, and nearby *Kata Tjuta*. *Uluru* is the Aboriginal name for what is also known as Ayers Rock or the Red Rock. *Kata Tjuta*, "many heads," is also referred to as the *Olgas*. *Uluru* is a massive sandstone monolith, believed to be about 700 million years old, in the heart of the Northern Territory's Red Centre desert, 450 km from the nearest large town, Alice Springs.

Uluru and *Kata Tjuta* are considered the spiritual heart of Australia and sacred to the Indigenous people. We remained in the area for a number of days to absorb the aboriginal landscape, explore the bush and outback, know the climate and immerse ourselves in the oldest living cultural history in the world, extending back some 65,000 years. Early one morning we drove to *Uluru* and embarked on a four-hour, ten km guided hike around the Great Rock. We saw rock paintings, water caves, lizards and birds; we also heard stories of the Dreaming, traditional stories and teaching tales orally transmitted for 600 centuries. As the sun rose on the never-ending desert, the rock was painted a hundred hues of red.

The next day we explored the alluring domed rock formations of *Kata Tjuta* where I was tempted to surrender to madness—as had a purposely lost Japanese tourist in the grip of a landscape-induced psychotic break—so I could remain among its captivating terrain forever. There are many kinds of gravity; the mind, too, is subject to its perpetual pull.

I have explored caves and caverns in Israel, Thailand and deep within the Rock of Gibraltar where Neanderthals lived for over 100,000 years, and also entered coastal caves along the cerulean Na Pali Coast in Kauai. Gazing into the luminous waters of the Blue Grotto in Capri, one of the most enchanting islands on the planet, one senses its womb of wonders. Located about twenty miles off the coast of Naples, Capri, a coveted island for poets, is also the site of Axel Munthe's intriguing Villa San Michele as well as prehistoric caves, some of which were appropriated by Tiberius, emperor of Rome, as his reclusive villa at Sperlonga, also referred to as the Caves of Tiberius.

In Jerusalem, we were supplied with flashlights—although on my first traverse, years before, it was candles—and rolled up our trousers for a forty-minute walk through the waters of Siloam Tunnel, also known as Hezekiah's Tunnel. It is a water tunnel that was strategically chiselled through the mountain to redirect a water supply into the besieged city in ancient times.

What's It All About?

On this swiftly tilting planet, every step produces a grand chord of harmonic reactions.

It is human nature to keep searching for meaning. It is not enough to be aware of only one plane of being, of only one reality. Just as there is an energetic relationship between the many strata of a biological ecosystem, so there are corresponding layers of discourse within all other phenomena. We may be enamoured by a monolithic, objective, scientific interpretation of our existence but it should not be allowed to dictate the full range of possibilities.

There have been so many adventurers throughout the ages and yet most dreams remain unfulfilled. As the ancient healer Hippocrates poignantly observed:

Life is short,
art long,
opportunity fleeting,
experiment dangerous,
judgment difficult.

I have shared a few recollections here with an awareness that all the words, names and memories described form but a headline that can only suggest the quest concealed within. And yet I also trust that the reader has intuited more than the literal words. Even if I have forgotten some details from these explorations, they still live in the unconscious, in the cellular body of the extended mind.

There is still so much to explore, to know, to experience, to be. I sometimes wonder why we have to take time to eat and waste precious hours in sleep. The world, itself, feels too small. As I contemplate the universe, I find that it, too, in spite of its relative vastness, is confining. I feel like I'm bumping my head against a low ceiling, and I wonder what lies beyond the Spacetime Continuum.

In 1888 in Paris, the astronomer and prolific writer Camille Flammarion published L'atmosphère: météorologie populaire. What remains most notable about this work is a single, wood-cut image known as the Flammarion engraving. When considering the evolution of our view of the universe, and how it has changed over the last century, Yosef Wosk says he sometimes feels like the figure in this illustration who struggles to see as far as possible from our earthly orb and feels confined by limited perceptions of the cosmos. – Ed.

Leonard Cohen at home, Los Angeles, September 2016. Photo by Graeme Mitchell / Redux.

RING THE BELLS

Leonard Cohen & Elie Wiesel

WE LOST TWO GREAT ONES in July and November of 2016. One was a reluctant prophet, the other a mischievous priest. Both would deny those titles. Both were blessed with the venerable Hebrew name *Eliezer,* meaning "God is my help."

The Hebrew name for Elie Wiesel, the most renowned author of the Holocaust, is *Eliezer ben Shlomo Ha'Levi v'Sarah.* I first met him in 1983 at an event at the National Museum of American Jewish history in Philadelphia, not far from the Liberty Bell. I was, at first, too timid to approach him but then I dared—mustering every ounce of "holy chutz-pah"—to introduce myself. I told him I would be moving to Boston in a few months and he, being the gracious teacher that he was, replied: "Wonderful. I hope you will come and study with me." Stunned at first, I soon took him up on his offer, eventually becoming his student and then a teaching assistant, later a colleague and, to a certain extent, a friend. That was forty years ago—the blink of an All-Seeing Eye when dealing with eternal questions.

The Hebrew name for Leonard Cohen, Canada's most famous poet and troubadour in the Tower of Song, is *Eliezer ben Nissan Ha'Kohain v'Masha.* Although we never met in the flesh, I communicated with his manager, Robert Kory, about bringing Leonard to the venerable

Orpheum Theatre in Vancouver for an evening of poetry, interview, song and conversation with the audience. The celebratory event—based upon the bold assumption that "Everybody knows that Leonard Cohen is the real poet laureate of Canada"—was going to be broadcast nationally on CBC television along with a dedicated CBC Radio *Ideas* program. I was also involved in an initiative to have him collaborate with such individuals as Steven Albahari, publisher of 21ST Editions, on a high quality, limited edition book of fine photography and literature.

In addition, I had a soulful conversation with Leonard's son, Adam, whom I met at a gallery opening of Leonard's artwork. We discussed the pressures associated with growing up in the shadow of famous fathers. Referring to his father, Adam lovingly commented. "No one man should be blessed with so many gifts: A poet and novelist, songwriter and musician, a lover, friend and father, and now an artist."

There is also another connection with Leonard that I have never mentioned. I paid off one of Leonard's oldest debts.

In the mid-1960s, the poet Seymour Mayne and a group of friends were in Robert Hirschhorn's Montreal apartment while Leonard strummed his guitar and offered them a repertoire of his latest songs. Seymour—who would become a prolific author and professor of literature at the University of Ottawa—impetuously predicted that Leonard would have great success and he would make a million dollars with his then-unrecorded songs.

Leonard playfully responded to this compliment by telling Seymour he would give $10,000 to Seymour's fledgling literary magazine if that ever happened. Over the years, Leonard and Seymour continued to joke about that pledge.

After Leonard Cohen's death, Seymour Mayne affectionately declared, in print: "Wager met and copiously acquitted."

Upon reading about Leonard's off-the-cuff commitment made among friends more than fifty years previously, I asked Seymour if he would consider my support of his publications and other writers as payment in full for Leonard's pledge. It was accepted and Leonard's debt was paid even as his guitar was laid to rest.

In spite of my efforts, I never met Leonard in person, but our intentions were never far apart.

In a turn of historical coincidence, Leonard Cohen, Elie Wiesel and I were related: we were all members of the age-old tribe of Levi. Our ideal appointment, as described in biblical literature, was to serve the nation as those responsible for religious leadership, as teachers and priests, musicians and guardians of the temple.

The Levites were given no land inheritance among the twelve tribes of Israel. They were compensated with tithes and a series of cities scattered among the others. God was their inheritance (Deuteronomy 18). Some of us, even after 3,200 years, awaken, often with surprise, to our generational calling and accept our millennial responsibilities beneath a mask of modernity.

These two Eliezers inhabited the archetypes of prophet and priest not because they wanted to, but rather because they expressed themselves so honestly, so deeply, with sincerity and authenticity. They were also recognized as such and accorded those roles by others; not everyone, but by many.

While Elie Wiesel made it his life's purpose to bring light and bear witness, a menorah (a ritual candelabrum stylized as a Tree of Light) remained one of Leonard's cherished possessions. David Remnick's *New Yorker* article published on October 10, 2016, just a month before Leonard's passing, described his modest living quarters during the 1990s when he moved to a Zen monastery: "Cohen lived in a tiny cabin that he outfitted with a coffeemaker, a menorah, a keyboard, and a laptop."

They both found peace in simplicity and realized, along with the Kotzker Rebbe, that "there is nothing more whole than a broken heart." That which is broken expands its dimensions, develops character and lets in the light. As Leonard famously sang:

Ring the bells that still can ring
Forget your perfect offering
There is a crack, a crack in everything
That's how the light gets in.

I like to think of Elie Wiesel and Leonard Cohen as ancient brothers who were born into modern incarnations, sons of the patriarchs and servants of the muse.

Leonard and Elie were brothers who never met, spiritual siblings from the same biblical family of Kehat, son of Levi, grandson of Jacob, the same Jacob who dreamed of ladders with angels ascending to heaven, and who had his named changed to Yisrael—"because you have struggled [*ysr*] with God [*el*] and with people, and have prevailed" (Genesis 32:28).

Leonard and Elie were born six years apart, but with just a few days separating them in September. Leonard was the *Cohen,* the priest, and Elie the *Levite,* the teacher. If Leonard was best known for his music, Elie Wiesel was known for his words. And yet Leonard was also a master of words and Elie a virtuoso of song.

It is useful to remember that when we first meet the Creator in the Book of Genesis, *Elohim* is depicted as a speaker ("and God *said* 'Let there be light'...") who used words—physical vibration infused with meaning—as essential building technology. Those who labour with words, letters, numbers and rhythm—the storytellers and poets, musicians, singers and their songs—imitate the Creator. That is how creation was called into being; all the rest is commentary. Wiesel and Cohen sang such songs of creation and amplified the echo of the inspiring lyrics of genesis, as they tapped into their excruciating quest to know the essence of the elusive empyrean.

Leonard Cohen
September 21, 1934 – November 7, 2016

Leonard was at once a gifted, complex individual and a simple suppli-cant to the Lord of Song. Born just before the autumnal equinox, he came from a long lineage of community scholars and leaders. He could trace his ancestry back almost 3,500 years to Aaron, the brother of Moses and Miriam, the same Aaron who was the first *kohain,* the first priest in Israel.

When I experienced him in concert, I was profoundly moved by the sincere intensity of his expression. In the midst of a song—when he bent down on one knee, sometimes two, when he held the microphone in one hand and raised the other to his head, fingers spread as if in prayer, his hat forward, eyes shut, face in shadow but spirit aglow—I realized, "Here is the real *Kohain Gadol,* the High Priest of Israel."

When Leonard performed, Theatre was transformed into Temple; sacrifice was not of animal but of soul and, it seemed, the long-awaited redemption was no longer a future expectation but a present possibility. Simultaneously, there was always humour and humility. Leonard, the Singing Priest, son of Nathan and Masha, sometimes referred to himself as "a lazy bastard in a suit" and by his Zen Buddhist name "Jikan", to which he added "the useless monk bows his head."

One of my favourite Leonard Cohen stories was told by Dr. Marvin Weintraub. When Marvin was living in Montreal many decades ago, he heard a young CBC radio interviewer ask Leonard if he was concerned about his last name being Cohen. She assumed he might be worried if his obviously Jewish surname might attract antisemitism.

"Have you ever considered changing your name?" she asked.

"Yes, I have," Leonard said.

"To what?"

"To September."

In bewilderment, she blurted out, "To Leonard September?"

"No," he said. Followed by a deadpan pause. "To September Cohen."

Yosef Wosk and Elie Wiesel in Vancouver, May 5, 1996. Photograph by Dina Goldstein.

Elie Wiesel

September 30, 1928 – July 2, 2016

It is seldom noted that Elie Wiesel transmitted revered melodies he heard in Chassidic Courts in Europe. He also composed songs and conducted choirs and orchestras on rare occasions. If not for the horror of the Holocaust, he might have grown up to be not only an important writer but also a musical maestro. I once found an antique conductor's baton at an auction and sent it to him as a gift, for what is a conductor without his baton, a magician without his wand, or a prophet without his staff?

I had the privilege of studying with Professor Wiesel at Boston University for five years and remember, on rare occasions when words were no longer sufficient, he would pause in his teaching, place a *kippah* upon his head, and sing a *niggun,* a haunting melody without words.

"Music is my life," he said. "When I write I need music, and a very special kind. It must not be symphonic because I cannot concentrate with symphonic music, but instead it can be chamber music or choral music, or requiems, which are my favourite musical compositions."

I have referred to Elie Wiesel at the outset as a reluctant prophet and this requires some explanation. Most prophets were reluctant. According to a midrash, Moses argued with God at the Burning Bush for seven days and seven nights in an effort to not take on the mantle of divine messenger. Another biblical prophet, Amos, protested: *Lo navi anokhi ve'lo ben navi anokhi,* "I am not a prophet nor the son of a prophet". And yet, he, too, was conscripted. Prophecy was not just vision but also voice. It was responsibility, not bliss; it implied the imperative to speak out, to act, to warn, to challenge, and ultimately to console.

Elie was only reluctant in that he was humble. After the horrors of injustice, violence and war were inflicted upon him and millions of others, he spoke and wrote with the passionate voice of a self-appointed prophet, out of necessity, God or no God. In 1996, when he accepted my invitation to be our guest at Simon Fraser University, I introduced him as the "conscience of our generation." A few minutes later he called me aside and mildly rebuked me: "I am not the conscience," he insisted. "Everyone must have their own." I'm happy to report that many years later President Obama made the same mistake. He called Elie Wiesel, "the conscience of the world."

When Wiesel received the Nobel Peace Prize in 1986 as "a messenger to mankind" and "a human being dedicated to humanity," he explained his actions by saying the whole world knew what was happening in the concentration camps but did nothing. "That is why I swore never to be silent whenever and wherever human beings endure suffering and humiliation."

Just as Leonard Cohen has countless memorable lyrics, so many Elie Wiesel sentences ring true through time. "We must always take sides," he said. "Neutrality helps the oppressor, never the victim. Silence encourages the tormentor, never the tormented." Equally important and insightful is this astute observation: "The opposite of love is not hate; it is indifference."

Hallelujah

Cohen's lyrics on "You Want It Darker", from the album of the same name, released just a month before his death, paraphrased the *Kaddish* prayer of mourning:

Magnified, sanctified, be thy holy name
Vilified, crucified, in the human frame
A million candles burning
for the help that never came
You want it darker —

Hineni, hineni
I'm ready, my Lord

Hineni is a Hebrew word translated as "Here I am." Spoken in the bible by Abraham (Genesis 22:1), Moses (Exodus 3:4) and Isaiah (6:8), it became the classic declaration of readiness to accept the task at hand.

Another famous Hebrew word, *halleluyah*, first found in the Book of Psalms, is at least three thousand years old. In the talmudic tractate *Psahim*, it is described as the most important word used to praise the Master of the Universe because it is composed of a combination of two words: *hallel*, which means praise; and *Yah*, which is a name of God.

There are many names of God. Some kabbalists describe the entire Torah—all of Creation—as nothing but the Names of God. But this name, Yah, is among the shortest. In Hebrew, it has only two letters, the two letters through which the Upper and the Lower Worlds were created: the *Yud* and the *Hey*. The *Yud* is considered the most spiritual of all letters; it is written above the line and is the only one that remains entirely suspended in Heaven. The second letter, the *Hey*, has an opening on its side through which it is impregnated. It also stands firmly with two supporting legs on Earth through which this material world was birthed.

The word *halleluyah* can now be understood as "Praised is God," or as Leonard referred to it—"Glory to the Lord" or "Blessed is the name!" In the mystical sense, *halleluyah* means "Praised is the Creator of the Upper and Lower Worlds." When the word was transcribed into various languages, including Latin and related European tongues, it took on various spellings and pronunciations with some confusion between the "y" and the "j" sound. When the Jamaican Rastafarians exclaim "Jah Guide," its translation from the original Hebrew means: *Yah* will guide, God will guide, or, more directly, God guides.

In Remnick's essay, Bob Dylan is quoted as referring to Leonard's songs as prayers and said: "His gift or genius is in his connection to the music of the spheres":

> Over the decades, Dylan and Cohen saw each other from time to time. In the early Eighties, Cohen went to see Dylan perform in Paris, and the next morning in a café they talked about their latest work. Dylan was especially interested in "Hallelujah." Even before three hundred other performers made "Hallelujah" famous with their cover versions, long before the song was included on the soundtrack for *Shrek* and as a staple on *American Idol*, Dylan recognized the beauty of its marriage of the sacred and the profane. He asked Cohen how long it took him to write.
>
> "Two years," Cohen lied.
>
> Actually, "Hallelujah" had taken him five years. He drafted dozens of verses and then it was years more before he settled on a final version. In several writing sessions, he found himself … banging his head against a hotel-room floor.
>
> Cohen told Dylan, "I really like 'I and I'" a song that appeared

on Dylan's album *Infidels*. How long did it take you to write that?"

"About fifteen minutes," Dylan said.

When I asked Cohen about that exchange, he said, "That's just the way the cards are dealt."

Elie Wiesel and Leonard Cohen are no longer among us. We, however, remain a part of them.

I did my best, it wasn't much
I couldn't feel, so I tried to touch
I've told the truth, I didn't come to fool you.
And even though
It all went wrong
I'll stand before the Lord of Song
With nothing on my tongue but Hallelujah.

From a crack in Liberty's Freedom Bell to Leonard's broken island knell, and from fractured humanity forever maimed by its failings to the soulful outpouring of two Eliezers, the world is a better place, a more noble endeavour, for their having passed this way. They, like us, were both imperfect, both broken, both striving for wholeness: that's how the light got in.

We are now free to imagine the spirits of these two Eliezers together in celestial conversation, singing and writing, the mysteries revealed, harmonizing, at last, on the Secret Chord.

Their searching lives may be over, but their posthumous careers have only just begun.

This text has been adapted from a memorial address and formal eulogy, "Two Eliezers: A Singing Priest and a Reluctant Prophet Among Us, A Tribute for Leonard Cohen and Elie Wiesel" presented by Yosef Wosk on

December 11, 2016, at the Jewish Community Centre, Vancouver. A menorah was lit and the audience was invited to recite the Kaddish—the traditional memorial prayer—for the two Eliezers. Wosk also generated an exhibition in the JCC's Zack Gallery from his personal collection of original artworks by Leonard Cohen, and encouraged and co-curated a memorial website at memoriesofleonard.com.

Claude Lévi-Strauss' cane, Paris, 2006. Photo by Yosef Wosk.

CLAUDE LÉVI-STRAUSS

On the Road to Psychogeography

Having spent considerable time studying the indigenous cultures of the Pacific Northwest of Canada, Claude Lévi-Strauss was one of the leading scholars and academics who gave voice to what had been a silent language of hidden meaning, a science of mythology.

IN 2006, I WAS ABLE TO RETURN to the City of Light and visit the French anthropologist and ethnologist Claude Lévi-Strauss, revered as one of the founders of modern anthropology.

Born in Belgium to French-Jewish parents, Lévi-Strauss was widely regarded as one of the most venerable sages of the academic world. He had visited British Columbia on several occasions to contemplate indigenous culture. Thrice married, he would die in Paris, in 2009, just a few weeks before his 101st birthday.

In retrospect, I can now see how, just as my father had guided me as a traveller when I was fourteen, Claude Lévi-Strauss was one of the major influences who had guided me towards psychogeography.

I first heard of Lévi-Strauss in 1970 when I took an introductory class in anthropology at the University of British Columbia (UBC). Our professors were Pierre Maranda and Elli Kongas Maranda. As irreverent undergraduates we referred to them as "the Maranda twins."

Under the Marandas' guidance, Lévi-Strauss became an iconic figure for me, one of those rare scholars who also took on the mantle of the heroic.

Lévi-Strauss' writings were not only cited for their contributions to the social sciences, but also to literature. For example, the jury of the *Prix Goncourt*—France's premier literary award—announced that if *Tristes Tropiques* (Lévi-Strauss' 1955 autobiographical masterpiece) had been a work of fiction, it would have received the prize.

Over time, I came to regard Lévi-Strauss as a totipotential poet-scholar. Here is a sampling of his reflective thoughts penned in 1943 and translated from the French by Sylvia Modelski for *The Way of the Masks* (D&M 1982):

There is … a magic place where the dreams of childhood hold a rendezvous, where century-old tree trunks sing and speak, where indefinable objects watch out for the visitor, with the anxious stare of human faces, where animals of superhuman gentleness join their petit paws like hands in prayer for the privilege of building the palace of the beaver for the chosen one, of guiding him to the realm of the seals, or of teaching him, with a mystic kiss, the language of the frog or the kingfisher.

I identified with his genuine curiosity. His search for meaning was not just an indifferent, or even passionate, intellectual affair. It was characterized by the vision of the outsider who observes phenomena for the first time, with fresh eyes and clear thoughts.

Equally inspiring, Lévi-Strauss was not content to remain *l'étranger*. Instead, he cradled the people and their artefacts with such empathy and respect that they became an intimate extension of himself without losing their own identity.

By embracing a multi-dimensional attitude that legitimized both subject and object—that appreciated the rhythm between thinker, thought and object of contemplation—he revealed a creative, structural relationship between apparently diverse episodes.

Lévi-Strauss developed a system, a choreography of sorts, wherein the trite can be partnered with the transcendent, and a series of concrete manifestations emerge as reverberations of their complimentary abstract opposites. He gave voice to what had been a silent language of hidden meaning, a science of mythology.

This science of folklore had always been there, but we were not; we may have been able to sense it at times but could not see its shape, hear its song nor touch its fanning feathers.

Lévi-Strauss was known as a seeker with immense patience; spending decades in consternation over the meaning of a carved pipe, a forest song or the fragment of an anomalous story.

My two travel companions for this pilgrimage to Paris were Kwakwa̱-ka̱'wakw (Kwakiutl) First Nations Chief William T. Cranmer and the transplanted, French anthropologist Guy Buchholtzer. On the surface, we three were a strange group of travellers: the chief, the rabbi and the expatriate. But our shared excursion in June of 2006 to speak with the fabled professor made us feel as inseparable as the Three Musketeers.

Chief Cranmer, whose lack of pretence quickly allowed me to call him Bill, was a consummate representative of his nation: good spirited with a trickster twinkle in his eye, classically handsome, an able administrator, a knowledgeable bridge-builder between diverse cultures, a respectful keeper of his people's ancestral traditions and one of fewer than two hundred speakers fluent in his native language.

Officially, he was Chair of Umista Cultural Society of the Kwak-wa̱ka̱'wakw First Nations of British Columbia, Chair of the Chiefs' National Committee for Language and Culture for the Assembly of First Nations of Canada, and Chief of Namgis of First Nation. Wherever we went, Chief Cranmer served as an affable magnet: his quiet authority and patient charisma filled the room.

A former physicist and French naval veteran, Guy Buchholtzer, however, was the leader of our expedition. Having moved to British Columbia several years previously to work with the First Nations, he was an anthropologist and former student of Lévi-Strauss. Of course, he spoke French, knew the culture, and where it was we were headed.

At the time, Buchholtzer was the Scholar-in-Residence of the Canadian Academy of Independent Scholars, an organization that I founded. Buchholtzer was both a persistent character and a Gallic romantic who had looked deeply into the opposing forces that inhabit human souls and could arrange a meeting, with anyone anywhere, when everyone else had given up and gone home.

A self-styled psychogeographer, former congregational rabbi and director of Interdisciplinary Programs in Continuing Studies at Simon Fraser University, I was the enthusiast who takes himself too seriously at times, wrestling with angels and sacrificing himself in a search for an encounter with the infinite *Ain Sof*, face to invisible face. In short, I may have been that person in the trio that Lévi-Strauss least needed to meet. And so off we naively went, like some numinous troika from *Yenne Velt* (*the World to Come; a far away place*), a band of triangulated emissaries on a mission to engage representatives of high culture in France (including UNESCO, Canadian Embassy and the European Academy of Arts & Sciences), the apogee of which would be our meeting with Lévi-Strauss.

Since the shaman could no longer come to the woods, we brought the embers home to him.

Our delegation had two main goals. The first was one of thanksgiving, to pay tribute to Lévi-Strauss and to honour his respectful interest in First Nations' cultures of the Americas over the preceding sixty-five years. We appreciated that he was widely perceived as a living legend. Our second purpose was to gain his approbation for our work of collecting actual or virtual international archival records dealing with First Nations cultures over the past century.

In addition, we were messengers for a series of greetings from Canadian dignitaries.

Madame Monique Lévi-Strauss greeted us at the door.

I felt a collage of feelings upon finally entering the apartment in the 7th arrondissement. The couple lived in the vicinity of the Eiffel Tower and the new Musée du Quai Branly, an institution that was decidedly influenced by Lévi-Strauss' argument that the arts and civilizations of Africa, Asia, Oceania and the Americas should not be presented merely as ethnographic exhibits but rather as dynamic expressions of living cultures, to be acknowledged for their own aesthetic qualities equal to European culture.

As we stood in the foyer, I was drawn to take photographs of two seemingly banal items: the cane and the kitchen. It was only later that I realized the symbolic value attached to these objects.

The kitchen photograph was deliciously ironic, for here was *la cuisine,* the literal cookery of the author of *The Raw and the Cooked,* one of the seminal works of structuralist anthropology which was published by Lévi-Strauss in 1964.

The second picture of the august explorer's weathered wood cane hanging from a brass coat hook, also took on meta-meaning. It came to symbolize his life: it was a wand and staff, stick or baton; it was also sceptre and sword, support and reward for a long life well-lived.

Two additional tensions defined the background situation: we were painfully aware of the preciousness of our short time together and, in the sweltering heat, I was half-afraid that if Lévi-Strauss didn't faint, I certainly would.

Out of a sense of respect, I would refrain from taking more pictures. I did not want to turn our host into an exotic *objet d'art* that we had come to observe. Some of the best photographs were therefore the ones that we did not take with a camera but were inscribed in our memories.

A half-moment later we were led into an adjoining parlour to meet the man himself. At ninety-eight, he was somewhat frail but he was filled with genuine enthusiasm and a welcoming kindness that helped to assuage our anxiety.

As the introductions were handled by Guy, for a few self-conscious seconds I wondered what I represented to him: an inconvenient interloper? I imagined Lévi-Strauss would be averse to pomp and circumstance, probably someone quickly bored by stilted and polite conversation. If he wasn't ensconced behind a table full of books and artefacts, I could fancifully envision him with a parrot on his shoulder and a monkey clinging to his leg, perhaps visiting an indigenous tribe deep in the Amazonian jungle or in a Pacific Northwest old-growth forest, pondering totem poles.

The room—a combination living room and library distinguished by large windows on one wall and an antique *tangka* on another—was lined floor to ceiling with a lifetime of research as well as with relics from the four corners of an astonishing earth.

We spoke about many things before Chief Cranmer reappeared in full regalia. The chief drummed and chanted two proprietary ritual songs in honour of Lévi-Strauss before bestowing upon him an Indigenous name and gifting him with a unique appliquéd vest.

We then presented our host with various missives from Canada including letters from former federal Cabinet Minister Stephen Owen, Assembly of First Nations National Chief Phil Fontaine, Simon Fraser University President Michael Stevenson, and Anthony Shelton, Director of the UBC Museum of Anthropology. Our final presentation to *le professeur* was a letter of appreciation for his lifetime of accomplishments and a description of our work as independent scholars.

At this juncture, I hesitatingly asked him if he would honour us by consenting to become the first Distinguished Patron of the Canadian Academy of Independent Scholars. As I handed him a beautifully designed certificate, he lowered his head and acquiesced, saying: "It is you who honour me. Thank you."

In the days preceding our visit, I scoured Parisian bookshops for a fine volume of Lévi-Strauss' writings so that he might inscribe it for me. I was getting discouraged until *eureka!*—I found a first edition of *La Pensée sauvage* in a rare books *librairie* near the *Jardin du Luxembourg*. When I showed it to the author, he immediately smiled in approval and proceeded to write a gracious dedication.

I knew that Lévi-Strauss was Jewish but I did not discover until two years later that his maternal grandfather, Emile Lévy, had been chief rabbi of Versailles. I had also heard that he, himself, was staunchly secular. I didn't know if what I was about to say next would be considered irreverent but this was my only opportunity and so I dared express it....

I playfully commented that not only did Chief Cranmer and the First Nations have tribes, but so did the Jewish people. I turned to Lévi-Strauss and announced: "We, too, are from the same tribe; the tribe of Levy."

Everyone laughed at this unexpected pronouncement, not laughter of disbelief but rather of recognition that, somehow, we are all related. The Levy nomenclature comes from both his father's (Lévi-Strauss) and mother's (Lévy) families. My paternal family's oral tradition, passed on for more than three millennia, also confirmed our position among the Levites. My full Hebrew name is *Yosef ben Moshe Aharon Ha'Levi*, "Yosef the son of Moses Aaron the Levite."

Wanting to transmit an authentic gift from his people's ancient tradition, I sat next to the aged savant and asked his permission to recite a blessing over him. It is offered upon seeing an outstanding scholar.

As I intoned the Hebrew words, his body trembled slightly, his head humbly bowed, and he reached up with both hands to cover his head, as if with a *kippah,* as a sign of remembered reverence.

> *Blessed are You of the Ineffable Name,*
> *our God, Master of the Universe,*
> *Who has given of His knowledge to human beings.*

And then we—Claude, his grandfather and I—whispered *Amen.*

I concluded with a *niggun,* a mystical spirit melody from the world of Before-There-Were-Words. We then sat in silence—for the song had absorbed all sound—and we were left in a perfect, if temporary, vacuum of tranquility.

That afternoon in 2006 was filled with greetings exchanged, gifts presented, letters delivered, conversation engaged, tea drunk, songs sung, spirits animated, books signed and honours bestowed, as well as with laughter and appreciation in abundance. The reverberations continue to enthuse me.

I wonder what transpires when we encounter someone who represents the Ideal. It could be a media star, guru, politician, athlete, lover, or anyone who is somehow regarded as famous or important to us in some way. We tend to feel simultaneously judged and elevated: judged for who we are not and elevated towards who we might be. We often become more enthralled by our grandiose projections rather than being grounded by the reality of the actual person.

This is something of what I felt in the presence of Lévi-Strauss. It may not have been the *real* man that I met but rather the manufactured model in my mind. It was not the Claude who looks at himself daily in the mirror hanging on his bathroom wall, the one who knows his foibles and is humble for a reason.

Even though such adrenaline-fuelled moments of meeting the imagined master may be flawed, we still return from such encounters forever changed but always the same. It is a kind of shock therapy in which our evolution has been inextricably quickened. These encounters with the Ideal are one of the techniques our psyches use to seduce us into crossing the threshold of our limitations.

ПИНСКЪ. Б. Кіевская улица
PIŃSK. Ul. W. Kijowska

Prior to the First World War, Pińsk was in Minsk gubernia (Minsk province) of the Russian Empire. Between the wars, Pińsk was in Poleskie województwa (Polesie province) of Poland. After the Second World War, Pińsk was in the USSR. Today, Pińsk is in Belarus.

WHERE I COME FROM

The Old Country

I AM A FIRST-GENERATION CANADIAN and a two-hundredth-generation descendant of Abraham and Sarah. They migrated from Ur and settled in Haran—towns in Mesopotamia's fertile crescent between the two great rivers, the Tigris and the Euphrates, in what is present-day Iraq. It was there that they heeded a prophetic dream directing them to leave their native country and wander in search of an as-yet-unknown promised land.

Dating back to about 1850 BCE, in the midst of the Bronze Age and extending through the Iron Age, we can follow my forebearers' general genealogy for the next 2,000 years as they lived primarily in the land of Canaan (approximately the same territory as present-day Israel) and in Egypt. During a long history with many fluctuations and turns of fortune, there were two cataclysmic invasions that led to the exile of the majority of the Jewish population. The first was subjugation at the hands of the Babylonians in 586 BCE; the second was the Roman conquest and subsequent sacking of Jerusalem in 70 CE.

My paternal ancestors were merchants in Odessa and in the nearby village of Vradiivka (Vradiavkak), in southwestern Ukraine, on the shore of the Black Sea, not far from Moldova. The Ukrainian iteration of the surname Wosk was originally *Woskoboynikovsky* (or *Woskaboinik*).

In Ukrainian, Russian, Yiddish and Hebrew it was pronounced *Vosko-boynik*—meaning "wax maker," a profession in which my ancestors must have been involved at one time.

We are traditionally descended from the Israelite tribe of Levi, one of the twelve sons of Jacob. Levi was loyal to his family but somewhat of a firebrand who was rebuked by his father. Over the following generations, the Levites learned to mitigate their zeal and became spiritual leaders and teachers among the Israelites. Moses was a Levite, as was his sister, Miriam, and elder brother Aaron who became the first *kohain*—cohen or priest—among his people after the Exodus from Egypt in about 1250 BCE.

My ancestors were among the Wandering Jews of antiquity. Outside of some speculation, their peregrinations—where they went and what they did—are not known for certain. We pick them up again after an absence of 1,800 years. All during that time, in the many lands of their sojourn, they observed the traditional customs of the biblical tribes of Israel, to which they assimilated, to some degree, aspects of the host nations in which they lived.

Mother

My mother, Dena Heckleman (1917–2001), was born in eastern Poland, in what is now part of Belarus, in the town of Pińsk, in the Polesia region, 220 kilometres southwest of Minsk, at the confluence of the Pina and Pripyat Rivers. The town can trace its Lithuanian origins to the tenth century and by 1900 about seventy-five percent of the population of Pińsk was Jewish. Over the next four decades it was conquered by various waves of Germans, Russians and Poles.

When my mother was still a toddler, the Polish army executed thirty-five Jewish residents on April 5, 1919 and this event was dubbed the Pińsk Massacre. It was merely a foretaste of what was to come.

Prior to the Second World War, approximately seventy percent of the town was still Jewish but, during the Holocaust, most of the Jewish population was annihilated. Specifically, eleven thousand Jews would be slaughtered just outside Pińsk in a Nazi pogrom, in early August of 1941, followed by the creation of the Pińsk Ghetto. Over a year later, members of Police Battalion 306 of the German Order Police would murder approximately 26,000 Jews imprisoned in the ghetto, including women and children, between October 29 and November 1, 1942.

Interviewed in 2003, the Polish writer Ryszard Kapuściński, who was born and raised in Pińsk, noted that the death toll from the liquidation of the Jewish ghetto is ranked second only to the more notorious death toll at Babi Yar, in strict terms of the number of Jews shot by Nazi-led forces. Following the Soviet invasion of Poland in 1939, Pińsk and the surrounding area were annexed to the Byelorussian Soviet Socialist Republic. After the collapse of the Soviet Union in 1991, Pińsk would become part of independent Belarus. Today, Jews comprise barely 0.1% of the population.

I know much less about the maternal side of our family because my mother was reluctant to speak about a legacy of persecutions. Hers was a silence that spoke proverbial volumes. In 2007, I published the following words in the catalogue for the opening of a photography exhibition organized by the North American Council for the Museum of the History of Polish Jews. The event was held at the Florence and Chafetz Hillel house at Boston University and featured four hundred photographs depicting Polish Jewish life prior to the Second World War.

*This page is dedicated to my mother, Dena bat Shlomo Heckleman,
who, as a child of Pińsk, saw too much and experienced
too deeply to ever speak of it again.*

*And to my father,
Morris J. Wosk, who, with most of his family,
survived the Ukrainian pogroms*

to begin a new and vibrant life
in a distant, promising land.

Although they are gone and
their lives are lived,
still
I see
their
faces.

In response to queries, my mother finally told me about a beloved grandfather, Mordehai Lasovsky Ha'Cohen, and mentioned an Uncle Archik. She also shared a few girlhood memories about chasing dragonflies and assisting her parents making pickles that she then helped her father bury in glass jars along the muddy banks of the nearby cold river. She remembered sitting on Zeydie Mordehai's lap as he held a sugar cube between his teeth and drank black tea, and how he would tell her stories and sing to her. One of her favourite memories was when he would give her five *groszy* whenever she would scratch his beard.

She also told me about some antisemitic incidences that soured her childhood innocence. In one of them she remembered hearing party music streaming from their non-Jewish neighbour's house. She lifted herself up on the outside open window-sill and peeked in. Dressed in their beautiful dresses and impeccable suits, they were eating, drinking and dancing in what seemed like a dream to a young girl. She then listened more closely to the music and the song they were boisterously singing: it ridiculed Yiddish caricatures and joked about getting rid of the Jews. The trance was broken as she returned home, confused and in tears, to her parents.

Her father—my grandfather Solomon who later became a haberdasher—obtained permission to immigrate to Canada, to Edmonton, where he worked for three years until he had saved enough money to send for his wife, Mary (Miriam), and their three daughters: Dena, Dora and Marsha.

My mother mentioned, just once or twice, that we were related to the Singers, originally Zynger, as in Isaac Bashevis Singer, the great Yiddish author. His father and his maternal grandfather were both rabbis, while he and two of his siblings became published authors. My mother remembered meeting him once, in the mid-1920s, when he came to visit the family in Pińsk.

She also informed us, but in hushed tones, that we were related to Lev Davidovich Bronstein, a Russian revolutionary who changed his name to Leon Trotsky. He played a pivotal role in the Russian Revolution of 1917, became a central figure in the founding of the Soviet Union, and is credited as being the principal architect of the Red Army. In the power vacuum following Lenin's death, Stalin turned on him and he was forced into exile, first in Turkey, followed by France and then in Norway.

Trotsky eventually found refuge in Mexico, in 1937, where he became close to Diego Rivera and Frida Kahlo, with whom he had an affair. In 1940, he was assassinated by a Stalinist agent hired to put an end to Trotsky's threat to Stalin's leadership. Our family, including my cousins, were warned never to mention our kinship with Trotsky to anyone out of fear that we, too, might become victims of targeted violence.

Father

In Ukraine, my paternal great-grandfather, Shapsa [or Shabbtai], was forced into the czar's army when he was just twelve years old. This happened to many young Jewish boys. If families couldn't hide their children from the military abductors, they sometimes even resorted to maiming the boys by shooting them in the foot or arm in hopes that this would make them unfit for service in foreign wars where the chances of survival were not good.

When he returned home after twenty-five years of military service,

Shapsa was granted land by the government, a rare privilege for a Jew. In turn, he permitted others in the community to plant crops or graze their animals on his large tract of farmland. He also harvested wheat that was sold to neighbours. To this day, Ukraine is known as "the breadbasket of Europe."

Some of my father's fondest childhood memories were from his time on the farm. I can remember only one: he used to be assigned to churn fresh milk from the cows and goats. As it got thicker, he would furtively skim whipped cream, and then butter, from the churning stick in the large bucket. Stolen pleasures are sweet.

Shapsa and his wife had thirteen children, twelve boys and a girl. My grandfather, Yosef, the youngest, married his oldest brother's daughter, his cousin Malka. Yosef and Malka (Mary) Woskoboynik had only two children, Ben (originally Binyamin, Benzion or Benusa) [1913–1995] and Morris (originally Moshe Aharon or Misha) [1917–2002]. It was rumoured that there was a third child, a daughter, who unfortunately died in infancy. My father was born in the shadows of the First World War and the Communist Revolution of 1917. Although his real birthday was sometime in November, he changed it upon moving to the New World. The date he chose to celebrate was July 4, American Independence Day, a time he identified with freedom. He also named one of his companies Liberty as a declaration of emancipation from persecution.

At that time, Ukraine was home to three million Jews, about twelve percent of the population. After the Russian Czar, Nicholas II, was deposed in February 1917 and murdered a year later, barbarous Russian and Bolshevik armies, along with Ukrainian Cossacks and other nationalists, dozens of politically aligned militias, as well as opportunistic gangs, thrived in the lawless chaos. They carried out pogroms in at least five hundred different locales in the Ukrainian People's Republic, which was established in November 1918. Between 1918 and 1921, approximately 100,000 Jews were killed, two-thirds of all Jewish homes were looted or destroyed, and approximately 600,000 Jews were either displaced internally or forced to flee across the border.

Cossacks routinely raided villages, shooting men and raping women. When they massacred men in the village of my grandparents, Yosef and Mary Woskoboynik disguised themselves as peasants and were spared. Their two sons were told to hide at the bottom of a large stack of hay in a horse-drawn cart. The Cossacks rode up to it with bayonets fixed on their rifles, shooting and shouting: *"Zhyd! Zhyd! Are there Jews here?!"* Ben and Morris survived that day only because the bayonets failed to reach them deep under the hay. Another time these two brothers were hidden behind the firewood stacked above and behind their home's large central oven as the enemy searched for victims. They survived, once again, but the trauma never left them.

The Spanish Flu killed millions throughout Europe from February 1918 to April 1920. The Communist paradise imagined by Marx, then promised by Lenin, was a façade for Jews, who were forbidden to attend synagogue, pray or study Hebrew. "Most of what I remember about my first ten years of life," Morris Wosk would tell his children, was that, "I had no toys, no childhood, and that I was always looking over my shoulder. I was afraid to walk the streets."

On another occasion, a militia stormed the town and arrested all the Jewish men, my grandfather, Yosef Woskoboynik, among them. They were herded to the local *taverna* and lined up against the wall. Every second one was to be shot. Just before the firing squad murdered the men, my grandmother, Malka, managed to bribe a former, non-Jewish neighbour, a policeman, who removed her husband, Yosef, from the lineup. Spared execution but frightened almost to death, his hair turned white overnight. Realizing they might not escape death the next time, they immediately began planning their escape from the Old Country.

Terrorism against Jewish targets would pain my father deeply for the rest of his life, prompting his determination to work on behalf of the reborn State of Israel. He never forgot the many relatives who had remained behind and perished as a result of Stalinist policies and purges, or else during the Holocaust perpetrated by the German Nazis and their collaborators, an unimaginable industrial-scale orgy of torture and murder that dwarfed the Ukrainian pogroms. Madness had become the new normal. Jews, as so often in the past, along with millions of others, became innocent victims of twisted ideologies that justified, even celebrated, such atrocities, including the killing of one-and-a-half million Jewish children.

All this brings to mind the searing words of Haim Nahman Bialik (1873–1934), born in the district of Volhynia in the Russian Empire and who lived in Odessa for many years. He later immigrated to pre-state Israel and became affectionately known as the National Poet. His epic lament, "The City of Slaughter," was written in Hebrew in the aftermath of the 1903 Kishinev pogrom. Here is an excerpt:

Arise and go now to the city of slaughter,
Wind your way into its courtyards;
There with your own hand touch,
And with the eyes of your [aching] head
Behold on tree, on stone, on fence, on plastered walls,
The spattered blood and dried brains of the dead.
It is they.

Splinters of broken glass burn with a diamond fire —
God sent everything at once,
Everyone feasted together:
The sun, and the spring, and the red massacre.
Rise, flee to the desert!
With impotent rage, your deformed heart!
Shed your tears upon barren boulder!
And send your bitter cry into the storm!

My grandparents were fortunate in having a relative already living in

Vancouver and so in the summer of 1928 they proceeded with plans for escaping from the chaotic hell their once-idyllic life had become. They had to be careful, however, not to arouse suspicion from the Bolshevik authorities for fear of being arrested as counter-revolutionaries. Emigration meant they would be forced to abandon their farm and an apartment building they owned in Odessa, without compensation.

The night before they were finally able to flee from Ukraine and the Soviet Union, my grandparents, uncle and father gathered in their basement for the last time, where they threw thousands of rubles into the burning furnace. There was dignity to be gained by assuring themselves their persecutors would not become beneficiaries of their plight.

In preparation for their escape from Odessa (a name that derives from the Greek, *Odusseia,* and is related to odyssey—implying a long journey), the Wosk family did risk one rebellious, death-defying act: Mary Woskoboynik sewed a small diamond into the lapel of the jacket worn by her youngest son, Moshe Aharon, because the youngest was least likely to be searched.

Over the course of the next six weeks of their overland journey, they stayed in a transit camp in Riga, Latvia. "Even though we had legitimate passports," my father later recalled, "we knew we could be shot or turned back at any time."

During the weeks that followed at sea, as the family huddled in the furnace room of a freighter as they crossed the Atlantic, my father served as the custodian for the precious diamond. During this 13,000-kilometre exodus in search of the new promised land of peace and freedom, the family could only carry with them a few personal belongings—including a silver Art Nouveau Shabbat candelabrum and a classic samovar (a device in which burning charcoal is inserted in a central vertical tube that, in turn, boils water for tea). A hundred years later, both items are still in our family.

Vancouver

It was a cousin, Abrasha Wosk, who first made it to Vancouver, British Columbia. He and his wife, Chava (*née* Nemetz), helped other family members obtain visas to Canada. The Nemetz family had moved to Vancouver, via Odessa and Watrous, Saskatchewan, in 1922. They were able to sponsor my family's legal immigration to Canada in the same year that the cornerstone of the first Jewish Community Centre was laid at 11th and Oak in Vancouver. It opened in 1928 at 2675 Oak Street (now the BC Lung Association Building). A historical plaque was unveiled in April of 2012.

Abrasha (a Yiddish/Russian diminutive of Abraham) later became a co-founder of the Schara Tzedeck congregation, the Achduth Society (a free-loan society for new immigrants), the first Jewish Old Folks' Home and the first burial chapel. According to the Vancouver Heritage Foundation, "The Jewish community's early centre was located in the 500–700 blocks of East Pender in Strathcona. The earlier Schara Tzedeck synagogue at the southeast corner of Heatley and Pender survives today as condominiums; Jews first worshipped in a converted house at 514 Heatley Street nearby."

In 1928, the weary Wosks finally arrived at Pier 21 at an unknown port named Halifax. It's now the site of the Canadian Museum of Immigration because the pier received almost one million immigrants between 1928 and 1971. The Wosks were met there by a representative of the Jewish Immigrant Aid Services, who directed them to the train station for their five-day journey by rail across Canada. He gave them a salami, a loaf of bread, some water, a few dollars and wished them luck. Such unforgettable kindness from a stranger buoyed their strength immeasurably.

Acclimatization in outlying British Columbia—about as far from the pogroms as they could get—would not be easy. Over-burdened with an influx of new immigrants, the fledgling Jewish community of Vancouver would collectively struggle to make ends meet. It would get even worse

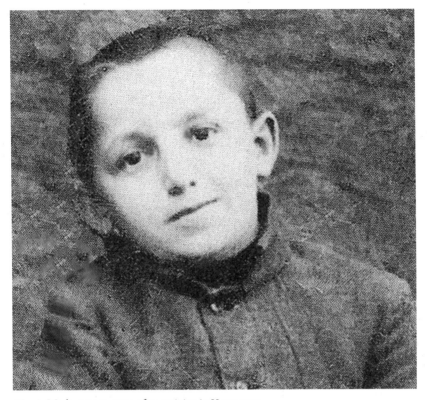

Morris Wosk, age ten, soon after arriving in Vancouver.

as the Great Depression made its presence felt across the world and un-
employment rates reached thirty-one percent in B.C.

After getting off the train in Vancouver, the family took shelter in the
home of Abe (Abrasha) and Chava Wosk on Parker Street, on the east
side of town. As soon as possible, my namesake grandfather Yosef would
find work tanning animal hides while my uncle Ben got a job in a broom
factory.

At ten years of age, my father spoke Yiddish, Russian and Ukrainian.
The next morning, after his arrival in Vancouver, without knowing a
word of English, he was walked to school and placed into a Grade 1 class-
room. The younger boys bullied him for his size, lack of language, and
not knowing anything about Canadian ways. He couldn't find his way

home after school and wandered lost in a strange neighbourhood for hours until someone found him.

My father later recalled, "I went to Macdonald School, at Victoria and Hastings, but although I sat with all the other kids, there was absolutely no communication. The other children were cruel and called me a big dummy. I was desperate to learn English, but I had no tutor."

There was one saving grace: baseball. Although he had never seen a baseball before, he soon excelled on the playground because he was almost eleven years old in a class of five- and six-year-olds. "Every time I hit the ball I got a home run," he recalled. Only one boy his age, Tom Carter, defended him at school; they would remain friends for the rest of their lives. I remember, when I myself was about eight years old, meeting Tom, and recall how he would exchange gifts with my father every Christmas. He would arrive at our door bearing a traditional Christmas cake containing dates, raisins, rum, mixed spice, cinnamon and cloves. I lifted it once: it was the heaviest and most solid cake I had ever seen, as well as the sweetest and most delicious. My father always had a gift for Tom in return and perhaps also helped him out in other ways. I've often thought of how the kindness of that one stranger made such an enormous difference to my father's life and therefore, by association, mine.

My father fondly remembered his modest bar mitzvah at the old Schara Tzedeck synagogue where there were barely enough people to form a *minyan* [the quorum of ten adult males required for communal worship in Orthodox Judaism, or ten adults of either gender in Conservative and Reform congregations]. In contradistinction to today's more lavish celebrations, there was only one herring, a bottle of wine and a honey cake. No gifts. Who could afford them?

My grandfather, father and uncle worked at a series of odd jobs before they started their first small business: collecting and repairing used pots and pans. They removed old bumps and bruises and polished the cookware until it looked almost new. They then sold them to make a small profit. Soon enough, they were able to afford a horse and buggy (*fer-*

deleh uhn agalah) to assist with their labours and expand the neighbour-hoods they could canvas. My father contributed to the selling and buying by calling out in a loud voice as they meandered through the streets, variations of: "Junk! Rags! Bottles! Whatever you need!" He also carried broken utensils in his little wagon to auction on Commercial Drive. He first worked as a common peddler at age thirteen.

Morris Wosk dropped out of school before completing Grade 6, at age fifteen, to join the family business full time. When a decision was made to open their first store at 1263 Granville Street in June 1932, for a rent of $35 per month, the Wosk brothers, Ben and Morrie, started by offering second-hand appliances and whatever else they could find at auctions. Their inventory consisted of an old oak table, one used Philco radio, no line of credit and less than $100 in the bank.

"We worked eighteen-hour days, seven days a week," my father said. "Even on Sundays we'd be fixing old chairs and polishing and straight-ening old pots and pans." The brothers were soon selling new applianc-es and furniture at Wosk's Ltd. where their motto promised "Nobody, But Nobody! Undersells Wosk's." They later added the reassuring slogan,

Wosk's House of Quality

"The House of Quality".

The Wosk brothers eventually operated a dozen outlets in the Lower Mainland and added a store in Alberta. Because of their numerous locations and ubiquitous advertising, a columnist dubbed them "the furniture kings". The largest store—located in the heart of downtown Vancouver at 58–62 West Hastings with adjacent warehouse space at 41 West Pender connected by a bridge across the back alley—was the location of "Mr. Ben" and "Mr. Morrie's" offices. It was there that all of us would gather every summer to watch what was for me, as a child, the magical Pacific National Exhibition parade with glittering floats, comic clowns and marching bands.

I also worked at the West Hastings store selling small appliances and assembling furniture when I was a teenager. After working at the store before Christmas one year, I took my hard-earned wages and purchased my first two albums: Ray Charles' *Greatest Hits* (1962) featuring "Unchain My Heart", "Georgia On My Mind" and "Hit The Road Jack"; and Roy Orbison's *Oh! Pretty Woman*. I was beginning to feel rather mature.

The Wosk brothers' first foray into real estate was in 1940 when they renovated an old house into four suites. As opportunities and expertise increased, they founded a small construction company and graduated to building a thirty-two-suite apartment building. Their apartment projects

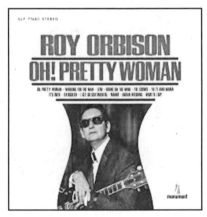

would become quickly identifiable around the city due to their integration of distinctive blue Italian tiles sourced from eastern Canada.

In 1946, my father Morris married my mother Dena, a teacher and gifted violinist from Edmonton who had received a gold medal from the Royal Academy of Music in London for obtaining the highest marks in Canada in her violin exams. She also liked to study scripture and became fluent in Hebrew, her fourth language. They would remain married for fifty-four years and raise four children: Miriam, me, Mordehai and Ken.

As a gift to my mother on their twenty-fifth wedding anniversary, my father paid for the construction of the Beit Wosk Community Centre in Ashkelon, Israel. It encompassed a musicology centre, a synagogue, an auditorium, activity rooms and major youth, seniors and arts programs. After my mother passed away in 2000, I arranged for the family to contribute funds to have the Dena Wosk School of Performing Arts at the Jewish Community Centre named after her. Expertly managed by Dana Camil Hewitt for the past twenty-five years, it has blossomed into one of the most successful performing arts schools in the city.

In 1962, at age forty-five, my father announced a major rental project at 1395 Beach, in the West End, only surpassed locally, in size, by the 234-suite Parkview Towers, west of the Burrard Bridge in Kitsilano. "The luxury 11-storey Surfside building," *The Vancouver Sun* reported, "overlooks Sunset Beach. With rents ranging from $90 to a maximum of $150, it could be a pacesetter among view apartment buildings. The 90-suite block is due to open March 1st."

My father understood media more than his brother and spent hours each week preparing full-page newspaper advertisements and content for CKNW radio announcements. Their most famous radio ad was a lively orchestrated jingle set to the theme song from *The Wizard of Oz*: "We're off to see the wizard, the Wonderful Wizard of Wosk". He also had a knack for public relations and was a civic booster.

"Vancouver shouldn't be a hick town," he told the *Vancouver Sun*. "It should show off its skyline. There's nothing like a high-rise building to do this. Look at the B.C. Electric Building and the Burrard Building. People take pride in showing them to visitors. Nobody wants to brag about a two- or three-storey building."

The first hotel the brothers built, in 1964, was the 100-room Blue Boy Hotel at 725 Southeast Marine Drive and Fraser Street, taking its name and emblem from the famous Gainsborough painting. This was followed by Vancouver's tallest building at the time, the 32-storey Blue Horizon at 1225 Robson Street which opened with 218 units in 1967. These projects were initiated by their company Stan-Ken Investments, named after two of their sons, until the brothers split up corporately in December of 1968.

Ben took charge of the Wosk's stores and Stan-Ken Investments while Morris took possession of the Blue Horizon and the Blue Boy hotels, with other assets split between them. Each continued to expand their real estate portfolios with Ben building two more hotels and my father accumulating about 1,500 rental suites throughout Metropolitan Vancouver, including the 20-acre Langara Gardens development and Beach Towers on the waterfront near English Bay.

The full story of how and why the two brothers parted ways has never been clearly told, and likely never will be. My father told me his version of some disturbing developments, but I never heard my uncle's side of the story so it seems inappropriate to share a one-sided version. After an arrangement was made to split assets as equally as possible, my father came into his own in terms of business acumen, community leadership and philanthropy.

For an immigrant pedlar who had pulled a wagon as a child and came here unable to even speak the language, civic honours were important as signposts for success, but equally as proof of acceptance. With honorary degrees from the Hebrew University in Jerusalem (*Honorary Doctor of Philosophy*, 1989) and Simon Fraser University (*Honorary Doctor of Laws*, 1996), he was also appointed as a member of the Order of Canada, the Order of British Columbia and as a Freeman of the City of Vancouver—the highest honours accorded by all three levels of government.

In 2020, he was posthumously elected to the Business Laureates of British Columbia Hall of Fame. The citation concluded: "Morris will be remembered as a man of immense joy and wisdom, with a genuine desire to help humankind."

In terms of his joy, "MJ" had a wonderful sense of humour. After being interviewed at a community event by Larry King—the doyen of television interviewers of that era—Vancouver Mayor Philip Owen commented, with a twinkle in his eye: "MJ out-kinged the King!" After another event featuring the eminent defense lawyer, Harvard Law professor and community activist Alan Dershowitz, the guest speaker from Boston told him, "Morris, you missed your calling. You could have been a great comedian."

When his brother Ben Wosk died at age eighty-one, while on vacation in Honolulu in 1995, my father chose not to attend the funeral. Born in Ukraine, then part of the Russian Empire, Ben Wosk first learned how to fix stoves and salvage other appliances after immigrating to Canada. Marrying Lil (Levy) in 1937, the couple supported numerous organizations, both Jewish and otherwise, most significantly the Schara Tzedeck Synagogue on Oak Street, opened in 1948, where he chaired their Burn the Mortgage Campaign in 1953. Ten years later he was chairman of the Synagogue's successful expansion to add a religious school and auditorium. He also supported the BC Heart Foundation, Vancouver Epilepsy Centre, Vancouver General Hospital, Boy Scouts, the Shriners and other undertakings. Recognized as a Man of the Year by the Big Brothers, he was awarded the Order of Canada in 1978.

Seven years after Ben Wosk died, the *Los Angeles Times* reported that Morris Wosk, 84, "a Ukrainian immigrant who became one of western Canada's leading businessmen and philanthropists," died Tuesday, April 9, 2002, in Las Vegas of heart failure. But his heart had not failed him while he lived. He once estimated that he had donated $50 million in his lifetime to a wide variety of causes.

I don't doubt that calculation: he was very good with numbers, quicker in his head than any accountant armed with a calculator. The boy who had managed to help his family escape from persecution by carrying a small jewel sewn into his frayed jacket, had accumulated riches but never without acknowledging the necessity of giving back. He liked to quote his own father: "If you make 10 cents, put one cent away, give one cent to charity, and spend the rest if you have to."

My father never forgot his difficult childhood—"I know what it is to be poor and living in fear," he told an interviewer. "It is something I will never forget." He remained eternally grateful for the safety of Canada. Over the years, he served on many boards, often in a leadership role as chairman. These included the Board of Trade, the Downtown Business Association, the B.C. Hotel Association, St. Paul's Hospital and the Canadian Council of Christians and Jews. MJ was also a major supporter of education, of medical centres and social service agencies, as well as all forms of art and culture. He was invited to the White House to meet with President Bill Clinton, among a select group of philanthropists in appreciation for their contributions to children's hospitals in North America.

A lifelong member of B'nai Brith and Congregation Schara Tzedeck, he also served on the Canadian board of Yeshiva University in New York and chaired the Vancouver chapter of Canadian Friends of Hebrew University in Jerusalem. He was a national vice-president of the Canada Israel Securities, Ltd. and past chairman of the Israel Bond Drive and the United Jewish Appeal. Numerous other organizations beyond British Columbia also benefited from his leadership and donations.

Morris J. Wosk was also a founder and long-time member of the Board of Trustees of the Simon Wiesenthal Center and its Museum of Tolerance in Los Angeles. In 1996, Prime Minister and Nobel Peace Prize laureate Shimon Peres presented him with the Jerusalem 3000 Award, given to only thirty-six families around the world at that time. On the walls of MJ's office were photos of his meetings, not only with Peres, but also with Queen Elizabeth, Mikhail Gorbachev, Golda Meir, Yitzhak Rabin, as well as many other prime ministers and presidents.

From having to drop out of elementary school to help with the family business, he later created numerous scholarships for deserving students and funded many schools from pre-school through university (three of which he helped to found). As someone who used to jest that he graduated from "the school of hard knocks," his name will live on for his philanthropic creations that include the internationally recognized Morris J. Wosk Centre for Dialogue on the Simon Fraser University campus in Vancouver. He also endowed a number of auditoriums throughout the city and in Israel, including the Wosk Auditorium at the Jewish Community Centre in 1962.

When he was called to the Torah, he was Moshe Aharon ben Yosef Ha'Levi. Friends called him Morris or Morrie. At work, he was MJ. Grandchildren affectionately knew him as Mo. All who were acquainted with him were elevated by his spirit. He inspired the greater good of our ever-ancient and always-becoming people. His blessed memory continues to inspire me.

After my parents passed away, I memorialized them in various ways including naming libraries, schools and gardens after them. Through the *Keren Kayemet LeYisrael,* we planted a 100,000-tree Peace Forest in their memory in the hills just outside of Jerusalem. I also became the lead donor for the Pacific Torah Institute, Vancouver's first yeshiva high school for boys, where Morris and Dena's grandson, my son Avi, became a charter student. It was officially named *Yeshivas Tiferet Moshe Aharon* after my father's Hebrew name.

Upbringing

I was born on March 26, 1949, four years after the Holocaust, during which Nazi Germany and its collaborators systematically murdered more than two-thirds of the Jews of Europe, including ninety percent of the children. It was also just ten months after the establishment of the State of Israel. I, and those of my generation, took the reality of Israel for granted until we learned, as every generation does sooner or later, that nothing should ever be taken for granted.

I was raised in a traditional Jewish home where we observed a number of religious practices including keeping kosher, giving *tsedaka* (charity) both in the ever-present *pushkeh* (charity box) and in the community, celebrating a modicum of *Shabbat* (Sabbath) and holiday observance, attending *shul* (synagogue) and becoming active in the community.

I attended Talmud Torah, a private elementary school with a dual curriculum of both Judaic and secular studies. Some of my favourite years were nursery when the learning adventure began; Grade 1 when I learned to read and print; Grade 3 when I learned to write and we had exceptional teachers; and Grade 7 when, once again, we had excellent teachers and it was time to graduate to the wider world beyond the walls of what sometimes felt like a self-imposed ghetto.

Seemingly shy but invariably curious, I was reading up to twenty newspapers and magazines per week by age ten. Because my mother was an accomplished musician, I was forced to take piano lessons. Drums would have been a better choice for me; I was more into hitting things, rhythmically of course. I also sang in choirs and took elocution lessons as well as instruction in tap dance, and as teenage years approached, ball-room dancing.

By Grade 7, in spite of my innate reserve, my athletic talents began to mature, puberty set in, it was our bar mitzvah year, and I was appointed head of the House of David (part of the student council). Upon grad-uation, I was presented with the Citizenship Award, a recognition that surprised me: I favoured someone else, Kenny Garfinkel, who I thought was one of the kindest students in our class. This reflection brings to mind what Rabbi Abraham Joshua Heschel once remarked: "When I was young, I used to admire intelligent people; as I grow older, I admire kind people." I suppose that even when I was young I was attracted to kind-ness. Perhaps it made me feel protected.

During my first few years of high school, my parents still compelled me to attend afternoon Judaic classes twice a week. While I was growing up—and certainly when juxtaposed to others in the community—I felt embarrassed to be Jewish. It was a vague feeling, a kind of low-level guilt, for which I did not have words at the time. I felt like an outsider, part of a persecuted minority among what seemed like a care-free, normal, secular majority population. I'm sure that, as their eldest son, I picked up some sense of justifiable paranoia from my parents' experience with antisemitism in their birth countries that contributed to my sense of unease, fear and of being constantly judged.

I still bear the burden, as well as the blessing, of being named after my paternal grandfather, Yosef, who was almost killed in the pogroms and whose hair turned white overnight. Having to abandon centuries of life in the Old Country and begin again in a strange land, among his last words, in Yiddish, just before he died at age seventy were: *Es iz genug*, "It is enough."

My high school years were spent at Sir Winston Churchill where, besides academic pursuits, I also participated in sports and politics. I was unexpectedly placed in an advanced class for Grade 8, one that included both French and Latin. Although I love words, my grammar in foreign languages has always been weak and there I was, at age fourteen, studying English, Hebrew, French and Latin simultaneously. The stress contributed to occasional nightmares in which I'd wake up in a sweat for not knowing the sentence structure and word order, definite or indefinite articles, male and female constructions, singular and plurals, or rules such as "if a noun or a pronoun is used as a subject it has a different ending than when it is being used as a direct object." Similarly, "adjectives change their endings to match the noun they are modifying and that noun's use in a sentence." See what I mean?

"Verbs also change their endings based on how they are moved to get across who is doing the action, when it is happening, and how many are doing the action." And that's only the beginning of Latin grammar. I'd also confuse one language for the other and stammer to put together a complete sentence without—under pressure to get it right—inserting a word from another language. It was all Greek to me!

All this was before the advent of more enlightened learning techniques such as French immersion. Classes were intellectual torture chambers. I spent a lot of time gazing out the window, wanting to be rocked in the gentle arms of nature rather than being restricted by the accusatory discipline of nurture. Instead of glowing with the joy of learning I felt more like an inadequate idiot who could not even grasp the basic structure of language.

I thrived, however, in many other high school extra-curricular activities such as the Year Book Annual, graphic arts, music, dancing and dating. I served a number of years as an elected representative to student council, eventually becoming president of the entire school (numbering 1,200 students) in my senior year.

In sports, I was a member of the cross-country running team, and also played soccer, rugby, field hockey and was especially involved in wrestling. At one point I was ranked number three in the province in my weight class (142 lbs.). I broke my nose playing baseball and ended up in hospital a second time when I caught a floor-hockey stick on the tip of my nose and had to be operated on for a deviated septum. A third break occurred in the midst of a rugby game but, by that time, I was able to snap it back into position. In Grade 12, I finally earned my Big Letter (C for Churchill) that was promptly sewed as a badge of honour on my blue school cardigan sweater.

I remained somewhat active in sports for another year but as I got more deeply involved in university life my attention increasingly turned to intellectual and spiritual pursuits, often fueled by the inhalation of what was then very illegal marijuana. The Sixties hippie revolution was in full bloom. Life became a great adventure: I was both the hunter and the hunted. Not everyone survived.

Early Travels

Although some of my earliest memories speak of wanting to know the world, to *be* the world, my gestation as a self-described psychogeographer began in 1962 at the Seattle World's Fair. With its motto of Living in the Space Age, it opened up new frontiers of knowledge, architecture and a sense of optimism that anything was possible. Riding the monorail, ascending the Space Needle and visiting the international pavilions awakened an inner courage and emboldened my resolve to celebrate with open arms all that ever was, is, or would be.

My next milestone, at age fourteen in 1963, opened the Gates of the World and presented me with its key. It was the year my father arranged for our family to embark on an eye-opening exploration of five countries, which included visits to the capitals of so many dreams—Jerusalem, London, Paris and Rome.

It began with our flight from Vancouver on a Boeing 707 (the first successful commercial passenger jetliner) to the metropolitan marvel of New York. I remember there being some discussion as to whether or not we should all fly on the same airplane. If, God forbid, the plane might crash, the entire family would be wiped out.

On my first day in Manhattan, I felt like an immigrant from a small town who had just been transported to a faraway wonderland. I stayed up half the night perched between pillows on the inner window ledge of our room on the 28th floor of the Americana Hotel, gazing in amazement at the world's tallest collection of buildings and marvelling at the millions of people who inhabited them. I wanted to meet each one.

A few days later—after visiting the Statue of Liberty, the Empire State Building, Rockefeller Centre, the Lower East Side, museums, taking a Circle Cruise around the island and eating in some of her famous restaurants—we boarded the *USS United States* for a transatlantic voyage to Le Havre in France. We then crossed the English Channel to Southampton where we disembarked for an extended tour of London. We visited theatres and squares, museums and palaces; I recall seeing neighbourhoods still strewn with the rubble of Nazi bombing raids.

From there we flew El Al to Israel, a highlight of our expertly guided travels to some of the cradles of western civilization. The instant we stepped off the plane and I took my first breath of the Holy Land, I really did feel like we had arrived in paradise. The sensation was enhanced by the intoxicating fragrance, wafting from nearby orchards, of Jaffa orange trees in full blossom. We met wonderful people on that trip including David Ben-Gurion, the first prime minister and founding father of Israel, at his desert kibbutz of Sdeh Boker.

A week later, we found ourselves in Rome where we were ushered into a front row seat in the Vatican's majestic Saint Peter's Basilica for the pope's weekly blessing. The saintly Pope John XXIII had died about a month before our visit and Pope Paul VI had recently assumed office. As he was carried aloft through the crowds on the papal palanquin, I instinctively reached up and touched the hem of his garment.

As a young non-Christian, unfamiliar with the Gospels, it was many years before I realized the irony of that action. Matthew 9:20–22, Luke 8:43–48, and Mark 5:22–43 all report the miraculous healing of a suffering woman who had surreptitiously touched Jesus's garment as he passed by in the midst of a large crowd. "And he said to her: 'Daughter, be of good comfort: your faith has made you whole; go in peace.'"

It was also in *Roma,* at a fancy restaurant in the landmark Excelsior Hotel, where I learned the true art of eating spaghetti. One of the waiters must have taken pity on my awkward attempts to scoop up the Italian national dish with a fork and knife. He instructed me to twist a few strands of pasta around the tines of my fork and then twirl them in the concave receptivity of a large spoon. After some failed attempts and much laughter, I managed to perfect the skill, tomato sauce and all. Akin to first learning how to use chopsticks, it has remained a favourite act of culinary competence ever since.

After Rome we visited the ever-enchanting Venice (ah, to get lost and loved in such a dream as this) and the French Riviera before our adventure culminated in *La Ville Lumière*, Paris. This indulgent journey not only shattered the limits of my youthful perceptions but made me realize that the entire world was open to exploration. I had a premonition that this larger reality would encourage me to dare to think for myself and that, in some enigmatic way, the planet was an extension of my body, or that I was a conscious, mobile appendage of the earth. The world was gradually becoming my new best friend.

"Travel," as Mark Twain put it, "is fatal to prejudice, bigotry and narrow-mindedness."

Sacred Studies

My studies have been a *pas de deux* of place and professor, of content and choreography, of travelling to learn and learning to travel, of being affected by the places in which I lived as much as what I learned from books in those hallowed halls. I studied, taught, lived and worked in Vancouver, Jerusalem, New York, Toronto, and Philadelphia, as well as in Somerville, Cambridge, Everett and Medford—four towns around Boston's central hub—before returning to the Left Coast of Lotus Land, aka YVR or Vancouver.

In fulfillment of Lao Tzu's dictum—"when the student is ready the teacher appears"—I encountered a number of master teachers over decades of studies in many cities, multiple schools and various subjects. As my inexorable pilgrimage continued to evolve, I was reminded that the Taoist sage's initial observation concluded with a liberating revelation: "And when the student is *truly* ready, the teacher disappears." I came to realize that I could learn from anything, anywhere, at any time. I found myself in the midst of a ubiquitous conversation not only with human instructors but also with the winds and waves, with flowers, trees, insects and birds, with rain and rocks, near earth and far-off stars.

The planet became an ally that grounded and nurtured, instructed and challenged me. I became restless in formal schools but still attended them, for it was there that I began to meet those kindred spirits who offered instruction in areas for which I was desperate for knowledge. I also developed a strong sense of personal discipline that almost destroyed me in the process of completing many courses of study.

Meanwhile, I continued to grapple with some of my uncomfortable emotions. The more I desired to engage the Ideal, to dwell in a universe of transparent gnosis, the more it seemed to stir up the corresponding depths and reactive inclinations.

I began to realize that life is a two-way mirror: as we explore darkness, it, too, looks back at us; as we dare partake of otherworldly forces, we also become conduits for their emerging into our carefully manicured minds. Just as one might practice safe sex on the physical plane, so one must learn how to insulate one's spiritual self, how to protect one's sanity.

Or, better yet, avoid the confrontation with insanity altogether. Even Moses, when he implored God to reveal more of its essence to him, was warned: "You cannot see My face, for no one can see Me and live" (Exodus 33:20). The inner and outer dimensions of human consciousness are too large, too complex, for us *not* to get tangled up in their evolving dramas.

We are both theatre and audience to our ever-unfolding dreams.

Undergraduate Studies

I didn't really want to attend university as I was restless to meet the rest of the world but settled into undergraduate studies with my comrade-in-arms, Les Ames, when an experimental interdisciplinary program at the University of British Columbia called Arts One was offered for the first time. We also enrolled in anthropology, film, theatre, literature and geography classes.

One class, Cultural Geography, was particularly meaningful. Among the phenomena we studied was how *Homo sapiens* had affected the world and how goods were transported from their place of origin to their place of consumption. I chose the potato, my favourite food, and traced it to its emergence in the highlands of the Andes mountains of South America. I discovered that there were over four thousand native species of the Andean underground tuber and that Indigenous tribes had eaten them for thousands of years.

When Spanish conquistadors introduced the starchy vegetable to Europe in the sixteenth century, it was greeted with suspicion and considered toxic by some, even being labelled the Devil's food. Although potatoes were soon adopted by the famished poor in Spain, they were still rejected by most other Europeans. Royalty gradually adopted the rather exotic product of the New World, and when Marie Antoinette, queen consort of France, began decorating her hair with potato flowers, its popularity was assured. It even became a symbol of love and procreativity owing to the folk principle of "correspondence" found in Sympathetic Magic in which the shape of small potatoes were reminiscent of testicles. Because of high yields in even meagre plots, it finally became a significant source of food and helped to alleviate Europe from hunger.

Over the following centuries, however, the potato became overly relied upon as a source of food and attained agricultural monoculture status. When the crop occasionally failed—as it did during the Irish Potato Famine from 1845 to 1849—a million people starved to death in the "Great Hunger". It was the cause of massive emigration of around another two million people, primarily to North America and to other locales in Great Britain.

As part of my final project for the course, I ate only potatoes for a week. I purchased and prepared them myself in ten different ways according to recipes I found in cookbooks or made up myself. At dinner, which I usually ate with my parents and siblings, they thought I was definitely taking my research too far. In any event, I was not getting along with my mother at the time and, in a fit of paranoia, I felt that she resented me so much that she might even try to poison whatever food she made. Consequently, it was a visceral relief to proceed with my independent culinary experiment.

I also wrote a mystical poem to the potato, claiming that it was originally penned by a Peruvian shaman. People do such things when their lives, or grades, depend on it.

At that time, I was becoming more interested in spirituality, particularly how it was experienced by other religions. Consequently, I studied and experimented with other religious practices including Hinduism, Buddhism and mystical teachings of all faiths. I spent my third year studying at the Hebrew University in Jerusalem. Upon returning to UBC to complete my degree, I took a number of courses in the Liberal Arts before receiving my Bachelor of Arts from UBC with a major in Religious Studies and minor in Geography (1971).

After graduation, I moved from my parents' home even if they felt somewhat forsaken. Only later did I understand that my leaving had triggered some form of PTSD, reminding them of when they, as children, had to abandon most of their families in order to escape with their lives.

I rented a one-bedroom attic apartment in Vancouver's Kitsilano district, home of the city's counter-cultural scene and adjacent to the beach, to the vast waters of the Pacific Ocean. I was already a vegetarian at that time but now that I was preparing my own meals, I explored the health food revolution even more. I also took a job as a janitor at my father's downtown Blue Horizon Hotel on Robson Street, also known as *Robsonstrasse* because of the ethnic mix of German and other European stores which had opened there after the Second World War. Then I worked in the hotel beer parlour as a waiter and bartender. I soon learned to pour a perfect pint of cold beer from the tap, one inch foam head and all.

All of this served as a precursor to a much greater adventure in learning. After graduating from university, I had given myself time to contemplate my future direction and decided to move to Jerusalem, in 1972. I would live in *Yerushalayim* (as Jerusalem is called in Hebrew) for six years: one as a student at Hebrew University (1969–1970); three-and-a-half years as a student at Israel Torah Research Institute–Talmudic Academy for Religious Studies, from which I received a B.H.L. [Bachelor of Hebrew Letters] (1972–1975); one year on sabbatical (1992–1993); and numerous other visits for shorter periods of time.

Y.W. or Allen Ginsberg's younger brother? At Bathurst Street apartment, Toronto, 1978. Possibly listening to In-A-Gadda-Da-Vida by Iron Butterfly. Photo by Eugene Goldfarb.

MY SEARCH FOR MEANING

The City of Gold

If I forget you, Jerusalem, let my right hand be forgotten.
Let my tongue adhere to the roof of my mouth if I do not remember
you, if I do not exalt Jerusalem above my greatest joy.
— (Psalm 137:5–6)

MY YEARS IN ISRAEL WERE hugely formative. They were mostly spent in the city referred to as *Yerushalayim shel Zahav*—Jerusalem of Gold—to indicate that it is highly valued as a spiritual treasure and because it is built almost exclusively of a dense, dolomitic limestone that appears golden when it reflects the sun. These complimentary characteristics make it not only the capital of monotheism but also a monolithic architectural phenomenon.

After two thousand years of exile—two millennia of living stateless and scattered in a diaspora that stretched around the world—the Jewish people were finally able to re-establish the country of Israel on May 14, 1948, just ten months before my birth. During all those long years as strangers in strange lands, the people never renounced their hope of return. They survived against overwhelming odds, thriving in some locales but persecuted and even annihilated in others. They prayed three times a day for the redemption of history and the return to the land of their ancestors.

The Torah Research Institute was at 2 Rehov Ha'Or (2, the Street of Light) in the Romema neighbourhood on a hill behind the Central Bus Station, one block from the Allenby Memorial. Known as Hartman's Yeshiva when I attended, the school's two main teachers were Rabbi Chaim Brovender and Rabbi Jay Miller. (The school has since moved and morphed into other institutions.)

I lived like a monk in a monastery for three and a half years at this Orthodox *yeshiva* (talmudic seminary) that had segregated institutions, kilometres apart, for men and women. It was there that I became immersed in traditional Judaic studies based on ancient literatures and millennia of commentary.

The more I learned and experienced, the more I accepted the accompanying slate of practices known as *halakha,* a term that is literally translated as "the going or the walking" but which generically comes to mean "the Law" or "the Path of Action." Although I had moved halfway around the world to the Middle East, my studies felt more like travels in time than in space. They presented me with vast historical and religious perspectives. The geography of the soul became as familiar to me as the primordial hills and storied gardens of the Old City.

We arose early for prayer and stayed up late for study. Every waking moment was dedicated to intentional learning. We recited a hundred blessings each day, dressed modestly and covered our heads with a *kippah,* also called a *yarmulka.* Some wore a formal black hat as a second covering. Our classes were based on Torah (biblical and prophetic literature), in addition to two thousand years of rabbinic commentary that expounded upon the Oral Law. Studies included *mishnah, talmud, midrash aggadah* (a type of inspirational storytelling) and *mussar* (ethical instruction) as well as *halakha.* We sang, danced, drank the occasional *l'chaim* (usually whiskey or wine), and celebrated Shabbat (the weekly Sabbath) either at the yeshiva or as guests at people's homes. We also volunteered for various causes and went on field trips throughout the country.

On Thursday nights, the evening before Shabbat, a few of us used to stay up all night learning. Sometimes, around midnight, we walked a kilometre or two to a bakery that was preparing tens of thousands of braided breads, called *challahs,* for the Sabbath. Baked by the hundreds at a time on moving shelves in large conveyor belt ovens, the fragrance of freshly baked bread drifted like incense over the Holy City and directed us to its source. We purchased a few loaves, said a blessing and ate one on the road, before rather mischievously returning to the yeshiva where one of us had a key to the kitchen. Trusting that we wouldn't be discovered, we sat at the late night table as if it were an altar in the Temple and took out a tub of soft butter to melt on our still-warm treasure. This was usually accompanied by instant coffee to help keep us awake, hot chocolate or mint tea, the *nana* having been freshly harvested that morning from the small herb garden just outside the door.

Jerusalem could not have been more consecrated or enjoyable as during those midnight meals. Unless, of course, the messiah himself had joined us in our forbidden but altogether understandable pleasure. Fortified, we returned to our studies for another few hours until the kiss of dawn.

When I wasn't getting high on warm bread and illicit butter, I was studying written and oral traditions in the City of Gold and making inroads as a writer, editor, public speaker, mentor, curator, researcher, art exhibit collaborator and a collector of books, art, and antiques.

I also volunteered to work in community gardens, in social services and at the Shaare Zedek Hospital during the Yom Kippur War in October 1973. It was then that I encountered my first dead body. I will never forget the silence, the stillness, and the unexpected weight.

It seems that when we are alive, a Life Force helps to elevate us but upon death nothing remains except "dead weight." The finality, the authenticity of such an occasion, of witnessing a last breath, is a deeply humbling experience. It is both a relief and a tragedy, a moment of mourning for lost company and unfulfilled dreams mixed with gratitude for having lived at all.

Since that time, in my role as clergy, I have visited many patients in hospitals and in palliative care, sat with the dying and held hands of comfort as the soul took its mortal leave. Many eulogies have been offered with a broken heart, prayers recited, rituals observed, burials conducted and earth reluctantly but honourably shovelled over simple coffins in open graves. *Yehi Zikhronam barukh*—May their memories always be for a blessing.

The war was a time of intense stress, as life in the Middle East often is and has been since time immemorial. Having been brought up in Canada, I had never experienced active armed conflict. During those days of uncertainty, I was an anxious nomad in search of my bearings. At times, we didn't even have the luxury to consider such things. People gathered around the radio every half hour to hear the latest news from the front— the casualties, battles, advances, setbacks—and what measures we, the civilian population, would have to take such as applying a coat of blue, semi-transparent paint to vehicle headlights and sealing windows at night so as not to allow light to escape and attract enemy bombers.

As most men were called to serve in the regular army or as reservists, hundreds of thousands of volunteers were needed to keep the country running. Food rationing was in effect as were daily curfews. Brought to the edge by the surprise attack of a coalition of Arab states, led by Egypt and Syria, we wondered if we would even survive for another day.

Two months after the war, while Israel was still reeling from the aftermath and recuperating from one of its deadliest conflicts, a Hanukkah celebration and memorial gathering was held at the Israel Torah Research Institute, ITRI, located in Beit Safafa, southeast Jerusalem. Surprisingly, I was asked to represent our much smaller yeshiva at the event. My address—in English mixed with Hebrew and a smattering of talmudic Aramaic—was delivered before an assemblage of hundreds of students and colleagues as well as august rabbinical sages, esteemed military personnel (some wounded), and high government officials including the Prime Minister of Israel, Golda Meir. Although my words were well received, I was so nervous as a neophyte before the crowd that I hardly looked up from my prepared remarks.

Beyond the city, in times of peace, I roamed throughout the *Altneuland*, "the Old-New Land," exploring the Jordan River, the Sea of Galilee, the Mediterranean and the Dead Seas. I climbed desert mountains, hiked through pomegranate orchards, descended to the lowest point on earth and meditated among the country's venerable olive groves. I embraced the ancient arbors, slept upon their roots, smiled as their slender verdigris leaves fluttered beneath a gentle breeze and unforgiving sun, and climbed their thousand-year-old wizened boughs wishing for nothing more than to become an actual part of such humble nobility.

As a writer, I was first published in 1973 when I wrote "A Journey to the Heart of Tradition" in Hartman's *Yeshiva Bulletin* (Jerusalem: Israel Torah Research Institute). As a nascent religious philosopher, I was then asked to edit *Petach: A Journal of Thought and Reflection*, Israel Torah Research Institute: The Shapell College Center for Jewish Studies, Jerusalem (1973–1975). I also contributed articles including "Torah Revelation: Then as Now" (vol. 2, p. 49–72, 1975), as well as "Can you say where I am and where I am not? Creation has arrived—It inhabits the universe" (vol. 1, p. 75–79, 1974).

Giving to support Israel, being present during heightened strife, and having been birthed there as a writer, has felt natural, not a duty.

In the following years, I arranged for the planting of thousands of trees near Jerusalem and in the Galilee, and sponsored the creation of over three hundred small libraries throughout the country including portable units for the IDF (Israel Defense Forces), collections for the Ethiopian community, as well as Spanish and other foreign language branches. Donations were also made to the national library as well as to social science, neighbourhood, history and holocaust libraries. In 1993, the Yosef Wosk Computer Center was established at the Bostoner Yeshiva in the Har Nof neighbourhood of Jerusalem, and 2001 saw the dedication of the Yosef Wosk Children's Synagogue Library at Shalva, an organization for mentally and physically handicapped children and their caregivers.

Besides personal journals, notebooks and extensive correspondence, other Jerusalem-based publications have included "Beneath the Mask: Fragments of an Estr Scroll", an extended prose-poem in *The Hidden and the Revealed: The Queen Esther Mosaics of Lilian Broca,* including other essays by Lilian Broca and Sheila Campbell with an introduction by Judy Chicago; Geffen Publishing House, Jerusalem and New York (2011).

My attempts to publish a digital version of the *Encyclopaedia Judaica* led to *Research Analysis Regarding the Publication of the Encyclopaedia Judaica on CD-ROM* (Aryel Publishing, Vancouver, for Keter Publishing House, Jerusalem, 1994).

In the late 1990s, I first imagined a book pertaining to Nachum Tim Gidal (1909–1996), a pioneering photojournalist, regarding our three years of correspondence between Jerusalem and Vancouver. The working title was *I Don't Need Any More Students, But I Could Sure Use A Friend: Letters to a Photoman.* The voluminous correspondence was later edited and reconfigured by Alan Twigg and published as *GIDAL: The Unusual Friendship of Yosef Wosk and Tim Gidal* (Douglas & McIntyre, Madeira Park, 2021). It received the Western Canada Jewish Book Awards Pinsky Givon Family Prize for Non-Fiction.

In fulfillment of a deathbed wish to the photographer, I also managed to curate, edit and publish *Memories of Jewish Poland: The 1932 Photographs of Nachum Tim Gidal* (Coordinated by Diane Evans; Introduction by Nissan N. Perez; Geffen Publishing House, Jerusalem and New York, 2020).

During my last year of intensive study in *Yerushalayim,* I moved out of the yeshiva dormitory and rented a small home in the picturesque hillside village of Ein Kerem—translated as "fountain, spring or well of the vineyard, or olive grove." This biblical town just outside Jerusalem is mentioned in Christian tradition as the site of the Church of St. John the Baptist (built over a cave said to be the saint's birthplace) and Mary's

Spring (where the Virgin Mary is believed to have drunk). I, too, entered the cave and drank from the waters.

An entire volume would not suffice to share all that I experienced in the ancient city that is holy to three major world religions. It was the locus of my dreams and for decades I thought I would go on *aliyah,* a physical and spiritual ascension to immigration.

The other place I fantasize about in Israel is *Tsfat,* or Safed, a mystical town, poet's village and artist's colony perched upon the earthquake-prone Galilean hills. The light there is so pristine and colours so vibrant, the air so pure and atmosphere so invigorating, the valley so deep and history so high, that every step feels like an embodiment of the six days of creation anointed with Sabbath's Silver Crown. It was also the site, in 1577, of the first printing press in western Asia to use movable type. It has some of the best falafel in the Middle East.

I wish I believed more in reincarnation, for it answers a number of theological questions and we really do need more than one lifetime to satisfy the multidimensional desires of our constantly wandering minds and broken, or at least wounded, hearts. I know of at least two people who finally moved to Israel when they were in their nineties. One of them passed away peacefully in his 102nd year. Perhaps there is still hope for me.

Once again, the hoary head of death hovers nearby and serves as a watchful, if impatient, guide.

New York, New York

Following my years of study in Jerusalem, I was restless and eager to stretch my folded wings. Possibilities flooded my constricted mind, aching for a renaissance into new territory. I considered embarking on an extended years-long trek around the world. I also imagined moving into a one-room rental apartment and working as a janitor. After years in the academy with its weight of complicated constructs and related obligations, I welcomed such relative simplicity. In addition, I'd be supporting myself, something that would help me feel more grounded and gain a sense of integrity.

Or I could become a Buddhist monk in an Asian mountain monastery; work in a book store or library (while dedicating myself to writing); maybe go into the family business; perhaps become a graphic artist or a baker; labour in fields and gardens; or work as a porter on the cross-country Canadian trains (I'd choose between Canadian National Railway and Canadian Pacific Railway, depending on the routes and conditions).

I went down to the Vancouver harbour and looked into joining the seaman's union and sailing on a freighter to a hundred world ports. Or perhaps I'd be a waiter in a restaurant (I had some experience including working a season in a Catskill Mountain resort in upstate New York). I also fantasized about dropping the burdens of life's responsibilities and becoming a blissed-out drug addict in an old-time Chinese opium den. To help finance my projected travels, I was very close to heading north to work in the forests or oilfields for a year. It was rumoured that one could make a lot of money in a relatively short amount of time engaged in such strenuous and dangerous work. In addition, I could save up almost everything I earned because room and board were included and there were few places to spend one's salary, though some desperate fellows lost everything to drink and gambling.

But after a few weeks of solo wandering in Europe, followed by a month back in Vancouver, then two months as a senior summer camp counsellor, I became humbled once again.

I realized two things: In many conversations, I heard the echo of my own words and realized they were empty—that is, I didn't really understand the depths of the religious doctrine that I was representing. Secondly, I valued the sanity of study and the benefit of having a stable social support system.

Instead of discovering the beaches of Goa, I enrolled in rabbinic studies in New York—at Yeshiva University, a talmudic academy in the midst of an urban jungle. To be accepted for these graduate-level studies, I had to submit transcripts from previous universities, request letters of recommendation, and take an oral exam to prove at least my mediocre grasp of talmudic literature. If I passed the exam then I would be accepted into the three-year *smikha* (rabbinic ordination) program; if my performance on the exam was anything less than stellar, then I would be assigned to a preliminary year of extra learning to raise my competency.

I knew I wouldn't have the patience for another four years of study so I prepared to drop out before I even began. In a turn of events that greatly influenced the rest of my life (and, by extension, thousands of others), I somehow passed the oral examination and began classes. I was feeling sincere, apprehensive and out of my league. Following a lifelong pattern, I once again found myself in a situation in which I was a mendicant, a beggar, an imposter among more competent practitioners. I felt like a combination of a five-year-old on his first tense day of kindergarten and a rejected Zen student, beaten by his master, who still sat at the gates of the monastery hoping for admission so he could engage in years of diligent practice. On the other hand, if I did not dare to continue seeking then I would have rejected myself even before being turned away by others. In spite of my personal failings and intellectual limitations, another part of me pushed on. It was for this whispered, deferential but insistent, voice that I existed. The darkness of doubt could have sabotaged me; I chose, instead, the simple but challenging path ahead.

Now admitted but feeling like the least of all disciples, I arose early for prayers followed by a quick breakfast in the school cafeteria and then spent the rest of the day, and half the night, learning. I studied what I could in rabbinic classes and with my *hevruta* (learning partner) while also being engaged in a parallel series of classes in Jewish philosophy, history, psychology and pedagogy. I had some master teachers but suffered through other rather pedantic offerings.

While taking refuge in a scholarly environment, I was simultaneously living in New York in a crime-ridden neighbourhood, among seven million people in a metropolitan area with numerous offerings of culture, sports, media, the sound of sirens and rivers of traffic. Waiting underground for the subway, I often felt threatened as if someone was about to jump out of the shadows and mug me. I signed up for weekly karate classes with Sensei Haim Sober and though I never made it past a Yellow Belt, it—along with my high school wrestling and a year of judo—gave me the confidence I needed to defend myself. With today's proliferation of guns, I may not have fared so well.

Every day in NYC was the equivalent of two days, or a week, in any other city. The sense of space among skyscrapers was both elevated and condensed; my perception of time was quickened and intensified. The pace was characterized by a barely contained recklessness, overflowing with urgency. Until leaving Manhattan three years later, I couldn't fully gauge how much the level of stress was magnified in The City. I became versed in the no-time-to-waste, direct attitude that emerged from that overflowing abundance of humanity It added another notch in my interface with the world where I, too, learned how to speak quicker, think more decisively and act more boldly when appropriate. It took me years, however, to stop completing other people's sentences, a habit, born of impatience, that emerged when speaking with someone who took too long to express themselves. I usually saw where they were going even if they couldn't.

I often considered quitting my studies. I remember diesel-powered city buses rushing through the streets crowned with illuminated, plastic advertisements inviting winter-bound northerners to escape to the idyllic warmth of the Florida sun. The cost was only $50 on some discount airline; seven flights a day. I had one foot out the door a number of times before somehow settling back into my academic web.

The final, written talmudic exams lasted up to seven hours each. After dedicating myself to a strict regime of studies, offering myself as a sacrifice upon the altar of academia, and following in the wake of a thousand exploits (so much true-life drama remains unmentioned), I earned my ordination as an orthodox rabbi from the Rabbi Isaac Elchanan Theological Seminary located on the Washington Heights campus. I also received a master of science degree in education from Ferkauf Graduate School of Education and Psychology in Greenwich Village. Both schools are constituent parts of Yeshiva University. The title of my thesis that concentrated on pedagogical storytelling was "A Teacher's Guide and Reintroduction to the Oral Tradition."

Toronto the Good

I moved back to Canada, to Toronto, where I rented a one-room suite above a hair salon and kosher bakery, on Bathurst south of Lawrence. It was my home for the next two-and-a-half years, from 1978 until 1980. Although I completed all my course work and exams in New York, my master's thesis in education had not yet been submitted. I became immersed in the landscape of story narrative, did research at the Ontario Institute for Studies in Education, took classes in storytelling at Lesley College, got involved with the storytelling community (most importantly Dan Yashinsky who would later receive the first Jane Jacobs Prize to honour his contributions as a storyteller to enhance Toronto's cultural life), and attended the National Storytelling Festival in Jonesborough, Tennessee. I also worked as a teacher at two schools, led a youth group and conducted High Holiday services for seniors.

I sometimes ate at old-school delis in Kensington Market, dated occasionally and thought about sex every day while searching for someone to marry.

A few months after arriving in the city and getting to know some of the locals, I was invited to join an eclectic study and social group that met once a month. It was composed of long-time friends, including two geniuses—one a recluse and the other an eccentric who stole books from the Toronto Public Library and could remember what you were wearing when he first met you 23 years ago—as well as four other very smart peo-

NAKED IN A PYRAMID

ple. All of their parents were Holocaust survivors and they, themselves, were born in various Displaced Persons Camps in Germany, Austria or Italy after the war. We studied biblical literature from an entirely secular and atheistic perspective. They had been too scarred by history to look at it in any other way.

Just as I was making plans for my next port of pilgrimage, I confided to a friend that I was thinking of leaving in a few months to study with a teacher and community in Philadelphia. My friend, Jack Eisner, whom I had known since Grade One, asked me, "Are you moving towards something or running away from something else?"

I was surprised by his somewhat challenging response. I thought he would be happy for me and unequivocally support my pending move. It took me a few days to recover, to respond even to myself, to his question. It was only then that I realized I *was* escaping from something—completing my master's thesis—more than moving towards the next chapter in my rather nomadic life.

I took a deep breath (one that would have to sustain me for another year), unpacked my psychic bags and, with considerable discipline, dedicated myself to another year of teaching, research and writing. In the midst of a storm of emotions, I somehow completed the thesis. In the days before computers, it was handwritten, given to a professional typist, then re-edited and typed again before being couriered to my mentor in New York.

Only then did I finally leave YYZ, that largest of Canadian cities. I crammed everything I owned into my first self-purchased car, hitched a small rented trailer to the back for overflow possessions, and headed for the American border in the midst of a January snow storm.

The little car with its heavy load couldn't make it up some of the long, steep, ice-covered roads so sometimes I had to pull over to the shoulder and patiently wait out the storm. My car—it was the only time I named a vehicle; I called her Betsy—was a compact, dark green, second hand, manual shift, 55 horsepower, three-door hatchback, Honda Civic with no leather seats (I considered such use of leather as being cruel to animals), and with hand-cranked wind-up windows (I thought that push-button electric windows were an unneeded luxury). I paid about $2,850 including tax.

Those were the days, my friend.

The City of Brotherly Love

I lived in Philadelphia for the next two-and-a-half years from 1981 to 1983, where I studied with Zalman Schachter-Shalomi (1924–2014) and others in the Jewish Renewal Movement, specifically in the B'nai Or spiritual community. I was, by now, an identifiable seeker, a lost-and-found pilgrim on the road to apotheosis. I had spent years learning text, practising ritual and conforming socially, but much of it was characterized by an emphasis on intellectual rigour and I had lost myself, once again, in the process. The real me was in hiding behind an incessant barrage of other people's thoughts. I had constructed an animatronic mask, one that looked exactly like me, a mask that both concealed and amplified me, but I was nowhere to be found except as a caricature of society's projections.

I thought I might rediscover a fuller sense of self in the City of Brotherly Love. Philadelphia is a combination of two Greek words: love (*phileo*) and brother (*adelphos*). The city was named by its founder, William Penn (1644–1718), who envisioned a city of religious tolerance where no one would be persecuted. Once again, I was blessed with master teachers, not just of the head but of the whole person.

I'd first heard about Reb Zalman ten years previously when a group of us were at a friend's mountain cabin in Whistler, in December of 1971. I was a recent graduate of UBC with no plans for the future and my whole life in front of me. I was also a drugged and drunk twenty-one-year-old, half-partying and half-searching, when someone introduced an article that spoke of Zalman's experimentation with LSD under the guidance of Timothy Leary. I had what Zalman would have called an "ah-ha moment." I realized that if he was doing that, then maybe there really was something to Judaism.

A few months later, on my way to Jerusalem, I decided to take the train to Winnipeg to visit a girlfriend and to meet Zalman who was teaching at the University of Manitoba. It was winter; the weather was freezing. Much of the campus was connected through underground tunnels so students wouldn't have to go outside to get to their classes if they were in another building. I found his office and we spoke for about fifteen minutes. I was immediately attracted to the way he was able to combine traditional teaching with secular studies and to also delve deep into Jewish mysticism. He also advised me that when I was in Jerusalem I shouldn't just be informed by one community but to *daven* (pray) at a different *minyan* (a congregation of at least ten adults) every Shabbat. "Try the Yemenite and Moroccan communities," he said. "Learn about the Hungarian and Bukharian, Italian and various Hasidic customs. Eat their food; sing their songs." I later learned that this was typical of Zalman's ecumenical attitude, not just within Judaism but also between world cultures.

I found an apartment on Emlen Street in the Mount Airy-Germantown neighbourhood of Philadelphia, near Zalman's large, old home that also served as headquarters of his B'nai Or Religious Fellowship. Over the next few years, I became an entrenched student of Zalman's manner of teaching, thinking, celebrating and related activities. I also became the Director of Education and Outreach Programs as well as the editor of the B'nai Or Journal. We recorded hundreds of hours of Zalman's classes both for use by his students and to transcribe for later publication. To help support myself, I also found part-time jobs at the Hillel Houses (campus organization for Jewish students) at the University of Pennsylvania (an Ivy League university founded in 1740 by Benjamin Franklin) and at LaSalle College (a Catholic university).

Zalman was a cosmic choreographer who celebrated multi-dimensional thinking. He was an iconoclastic thinker who navigated effortlessly through the Four Worlds, the Ten Sephirot and the Seventy Faces of Torah. I will share more stories about him in an upcoming publication on my teachers but here is a taste.

Aaron Levine, Simcha Paull, David Blank and myself were participants in Zalman's version of the *Dharma Bums*. We were privileged to travel with him to some of his presentations. We often passed a joint around as we drove the many miles between venues, something that both inspired our conversation and made the distance more bearable. Once in a while Zalman had to remind us not to exceed the speed limit so we wouldn't be pulled over for speeding and busted for smoking pot.

In this way we met Swami Satchidananda (the Woodstock guru and founder of Integral Yoga) at his Yogaville ashram in Virginia, joined with Sheikh Muzafar and his Turkish Sufis for Zikkur in New York's Cathedral of Saint John the Divine, and welcomed sunrise from the top of the Empire State Building in a ceremony (*Birkhat Ha'Hama*) that takes place only once every nineteen years as the sun returns to the position it occupied at the time of creation.

We also ventured to the New Jersey countryside, to the home of one of Reb Zalman's students, for a tomato. Upon arrival on a hot summer afternoon, she greeted us and led us into her backyard where she had cultivated a lush garden. She offered us cold beers and then picked a large, ripe, New Jersey beefsteak tomato from the vine and cut it into wedges with her serrated paring knife. I said the blessing—*Barukh ata Adonigh, Eloheinu melekh ha'olam,* "Blessed are you, Lord, our God, ruler of the universe, who creates fruit of the ground"—and bit into it, still a little suspicious and wondering what all the fuss was about. My eyes immediately closed, my body uttered an "mmm-m-m" through my closed lips, and I realized that I had never tasted a real tomato before that moment. Its flavour burst upon me, with texture, colour and juiciness to match. Every other tomato—indeed every other vegetable (I know, tomatoes are botanically classified as fruit)—that I had ever eaten tasted like dry cardboard in comparison. We picked another and shared it amongst us: it was a manifestation of Heaven on Earth. Amen.

Other visitors came to pay respects at Zalman's home. I particularly remember one somewhat mysterious guest; I believe it was the illustrious Iranian scholar Seyyed Hossein Nasr who had been exiled from his homeland because of the 1979 revolution and who was then appointed a professor of Islamic studies at Temple University in Philadelphia. A woman, to whom I was deeply attached, had just broken up with me in a letter that I had received that Friday afternoon before the Sabbath. I felt devastated; my body numb. And then, when I was cutting vegetables for the Sabbath meal, the knife slipped and cut my finger. It felt like an unconscious maiming to match my emotional pain.

Later that evening, after lighting Shabbat candles and sitting down to dinner (even though I had no appetite), a visitor knocked on the door. Zalman welcomed him, introduced him to me, and then the two of them went upstairs to his office. Perhaps it was Seyyed's Sufi training that made him extraordinarily sensitive, but an hour later, as he was leaving, he intuited my emotional state. Instead of just shaking my hand, he reached over and placed his right hand over my chest, upon my heart. I was surprised but surrendered to the unexpected gesture. I felt a great warmth emanate from his hand and the beginning not just of healing but of an immense sense of well-being. Even forty years later, whenever I place my right hand over the left side of my chest I feel noble, serene and uplifted. I often greet people, especially from Islamic countries, with a slight bow of my head and with hand lifted to heart. They know; they smile; the gesture speaks the language of the soul.

Zalman also taught at Temple University and sometimes I would accompany him to his classes. One day, as we were returning home, he popped a cassette into the car radio and said, "Here, listen to this." I sat enthralled for the next five minutes listening to the master teacher and orator, Jean Houston. After Zalman encouraged a few of us to attend Houston's workshop in Washington, D.C. I would remain her on-again, off-again student for the next seven years. Her words, optimism and vision continue to influence me to this day.

From 1982 to 1985, I was part of Jean's Three-Year Training Program in Human Capacities run through the Foundation for Mind Research that she and her husband, Robert Masters, established at their home base in Pomona, New York. Along with a few other highly trained faculty, they guided us to transcend our limited personas. The program began with about 120 mature students in the first year but was winnowed down to approximately 85 by year three. We met each summer at the rented facilities of Ramapo College in Mahwah, New Jersey for a month-long series of intensive sessions, and then again each winter for a week-long retreat in Pacific Palisades, about twenty miles west of downtown Los Angeles. Mentors kept us networked during the rest of the year.

In these sessions we engaged in topics such as depth psychology, archetypal fundamentals, the correspondence between human psyche and universal principles, the meanings of myth, interactive participatory literature, body and neural networking, body reading, hypnotism and other altered states of awareness. We learned how to access not just the five basic senses but also the hundreds of more subtle gates of perception that hover within, around and beyond us.

I became particularly interested in discussing the Earth as global mind, and translating geography, as well as the wisdom of classical civilizations, into visceral consciousness. These exploratory sessions helped to deepen my evolving engagement with what I later identified as the field of psychogeography.

At the conclusion of those initial three-year studies into the fulfillment of the extended mind and the ongoing birthing of the brain, I continued with Jean's *Mystery School* for advanced training in therapeia and psychosomatic techniques.

We met once a month for two years from 1985 to 1987, at various locations in the northeastern United States. A number of us also joined an expedition to Greece and Egypt to encounter the spiritual essence of bygone civilizations, exploration of cultures, sacred and secular histories, rituals, temples and ruins. Studies and elemental experiences with this outstanding group of instructors, along with deep interactions with fellow students, transformed me into the next incarnation of my peripatetic soul.

I extended myself further by signing up for something I never thought I was capable of achieving: a doctoral degree. For those of us who wanted to pursue advanced degrees, the Foundation for Mind Research made arrangements with William Lyon University in San Diego. Under Jean's comprehensive guidance, I proceeded to complete six years of part-time study for a certificate in Human Capacities (1983–1985) and a Ph.D, in 1989, in Transpersonal Psychology. The title of my dissertation was "Storied Reflections: Aspects in the Theory and Practice of Storytelling as an Agent of Psychospiritual Maturation."

Master mentors for my doctoral studies were Father Dr. Thomas Berry (1914–2009), who taught at various institutes of higher learning including Fordham University in New York where he chaired the history of religions program, and Rabbi Dr. Zalman Schachter-Shalomi who was also a professor at several other universities. Before I left Philadelphia, Zalman granted me a second kind of ordination, that of a *Maggid*. It is defined as "a traditional Jewish itinerant preacher, skilled as a narrator of Torah and religious stories."

Tom Berry was the kindest man I ever met. A Catholic Passionist priest and retired university professor, he lived in a rambling home in Riverdale, just north of Manhattan, on the banks high above the Hudson River where he also directed the Riverdale Center of Religious Research. A great tree grew there and that is where we often met. He was described by Columbia University as "one of the twentieth century's most prescient and profound thinkers." I had requested to study with him because of his work as a cultural historian, a philosopher of world religions, his profound engagement with the nature of "story" and his spiritual understanding of the shifting relationship between the Earth and Consciousness. He referred to himself as a geologian.

Boston Years

Harvard Divinity School

As my studies and experiential training in Philadelphia were coming to a close, I considered finally returning to Israel to go on *Aliyah* (immigration). I was about to make plans when I noticed a small advertisement in the weekend *New York Times Book Review*. It proclaimed: "An invitation to study theology at Harvard."

Intrigued, I tore it out but didn't think that I would be accepted to the program so I concealed the notice for future consideration. When I stumbled upon it again a few months later, I decided to discuss it with my therapist. She led me on a guided imagery session in which I found myself dressed like a British school boy in grey flannel trousers, a dark blue blazer with shiny brass buttons, polished black shoes, and a white shirt with a striped tie. I was sitting, intimidated, in the back row of what seemed like a preliminary class at the Divinity School. The professor asked a question but no one offered a response. Realizing that I had an opinion based on my years of previous learning, I raised my hand and offered a couple of ideas which were well received.

Coming out of the trance, I was relieved and knew that I could, indeed, fit in. Emboldened but still tentative, I began preparing my application for graduate school soon after. I did so while waiting in the mechanic's anteroom as my car was being serviced. Apparently, I still needed such a distraction to assuage my resistance, buffer my fear of rejection and prepare me to tackle my next audacious adventure.

A few months later, towards the beginning of a New England autumn, I found myself timidly setting foot in what still felt like the fabled Harvard Yard. It was there I would learn much more about Christianity, Central and South American native traditions, African tribal religions and comparative world religions.

Some of the major essays written in the course of studies included

"A Rereading of the Gospel Parables: A Second Chance to Make a First Impression," "Aspects of Healing in Judaism," "A Transpersonal Portrait of Moses" and "High Spots and Sacred Centres," my continuing foray into the field of sacred geography.

I graduated from the rarefied air of that Ivy League school two years later, in 1985, as a Master of Theology—*Theologiae Magistri cum laude*. There was an oral exam but no graduating thesis was required for the ThM. I only had to decide what to do next.

I took a job at a corner gas station. It was the best thing I could ever have done. It put grease on my hands, money in my pocket and connected me with the street once again.

Even while working or engaged in formal studies, I continued to attend sessions with a cornucopia of inspiring teachers. Between 1978 and 1984 I attended seminars with three seminal thinkers of the twentieth century: Buckminster Fuller in Toronto, Philadelphia, and Washington D.C.; Marshall McLuhan in Toronto; and Joseph Campbell in New York and Boston. This trio envisioned great perspective and celebrated the big picture. Fuller spoke optimistically about Spaceship Earth with first class accommodations for all; McLuhan about the meaning of technologies and communications; while Campbell, the literary mythologist, connected ancient civilizations with the present through an appreciation of underlying archetypal principles. And then, of course, there was the previously mentioned Jean Houston (a close associate of Margaret Mead) with whom I apprenticed for seven years.

Congregational Rabbi, Prison Chaplain and Hospital Clergy

When a friend went on a sabbatical to Israel and needed someone to take his place for a year, I left my job at the gas station and accepted employment as a congregational rabbi.

I was reluctant, at first, to accept such a posting. I felt that I was not yet prepared; not yet married; no family of my own; no deaths in the family so how could I empathize with tragedy, loss and the vicissitudes of daily life; in addition to an entire litany of other excuses. Eventually overcoming my resistance, I took the position at Congregation Tifereth Israel and moved to Everett, a suburb about four miles north of downtown Boston.

The tail end of a hurricane blew through the deserted streets of the city on the day of the move, almost blowing the truck over. I arrived on Friday afternoon and the truck was finally unloaded just before the Sabbath. Relieved, dirty and drenched from the storm, I was about to soak in a hot bath when I heard a knock on the door of the rabbi's house. There were three elderly congregants wondering where the interim rabbi was to lead the Shabbat services. I felt as embarrassed and as incompetent as I thought I'd be.

As it turned out, the hurricane had damaged the electric grid and there were no lights in the synagogue. Services were cancelled.

As the weeks progressed, however, I soon discovered that all the teachings of the past decades came flooding through me. It had all been worth it. What had once been a private journey now morphed into a communal caravan. We accomplished a lot that year including dedicating a library, instituting an extensive adult education program, becoming a regional venue for studies in Jewish mysticism, publishing a congregational bulletin, reaching out to the non-Jewish community and organizing adult bat mitsvah studies with a graduation ceremony for women. Healing, death and dying, funerals, weddings and counselling were also significant aspects of my responsibilities.

While in that community I also served as a chaplain at a State Maximum Security Prison in Walpole and as a chaplain for Jewish patients at the Soldier's Home and Hospital in Chelsea, Massachusetts. One day, when I visited the Soldier's Home for American war veterans, I went up to the top floor of the hospital where some of the oldest patients were cared for. Slanting rays of afternoon sunlight streamed through the tall windows of the red brick building and illuminated a few of the neatly arranged beds. Each was bedecked with clean, white sheets, grey wool blankets and the mostly comatose bodies, covered in transparent ivory skin, of ninety-year-old veterans of the First World War.

These were among the last of the survivors. I stood transfixed by the strange scene and reflected how any one of them could have huddled next to a comrade in a muddy front-line trench in 1917 and been stunned as their friend was killed by a bullet or grenade while they somehow were spared to live another seventy years.

"What is luck," I thought, "or a miracle? And why would a miracle be performed for one but death be declared for another? Or, perhaps even more disturbing to the religious mind, it was all just chance and carries no meaning. Is chaos, and not a moral universe, the new God? Certainly of war."

There weren't many Jewish prisoners in Walpole. I remember two of them but forget their names. One was Black, a former member of a Chicago street gang who was in for murder. He claimed he was a Hebrew Israelite whose adherents believe their self-proclaimed Jewish faith is part of their African heritage. I didn't question the legitimacy of his Jewishness—he was already being judged enough—and during our visits we shared contemplative conversations. I also brought him a prayer book, a Bible, an open ear and, occasionally, frozen, catered kosher meals with a double portion for the religious holidays.

The other inmate, I'll call him Tyler, was in his late twenties and had been in trouble all his life. We developed a respectful friendship and I arranged for requested gifts, especially clothes and a good pair of running shoes, from his family. One night I received a phone message from the prison that he had escaped by hiding in the bottom of a laundry cart. Within a couple of days he got possession of a gun and was robbing homes. He shot a police officer who was in pursuit and then took refuge in a home where he held the family hostage. The house was then surrounded by a SWAT team while police psychologists tried to negotiate his surrender.

As media swarmed the scene, a policeman next to me muttered in disgust: "They're all whores! Anything for a story!" I was called to the scene to see if I could convince Tyler to free the hostages before anyone else got hurt.

After determining where everyone in the house was and knowing that after twenty-four hours of no sleep the gunman was getting drowsy—he had already duct taped the weapon to his wrist so it wouldn't fall if he dozed off—the SWAT team burst through a second floor window and subdued him. No one was injured; he was handcuffed and returned to prison in a paddy wagon where he was sentenced to additional decades behind bars for his desperate flight, illegal possession of a firearm, attempted murder of a policeman, kidnapping and hostage taking.

During my year in Everett, I made heartfelt friends and tears were shed when it came time to depart. At a farewell event, I was deeply moved when the community presented me with an Appreciation Award for "untiring abounding love, dedication and devotion to our congregants and the entire Jewish community"—*Congregation Tifereth Israel,* Everett (1986).

Attending that event was a politician from the Massachusetts House of Representatives. As we conversed and I found out that he was descended from Irish ancestors, I told him how much I appreciated Irish literary and storytelling culture. He then proudly shared some rhyming folk wisdom he heard from his mother, and she from her grandmother:

Good, better, best,
Never let it rest,
Until your good is better
And your better best.

To which I told him what my mother used to remind us when we were children: "Please, thank you and courtesy, costs nothing but gains much."

After completing a year of substituting for my friend, three other congregations approached me to take the pulpit as their rabbi. I chose one, Temple Shalom in Medford, another Boston suburb, and home to Tufts

University. Once again, working with all strata of community demographics, I was able to help revitalize the *shul* (synagogue).

During my tenure in Medford we received two North American-wide *Solomon Schechter Awards for Excellence in Synagogue Programming* from the United Synagogue of America, the Association of Conservative Congregations. The categories were "Holocaust Education" and "Judaica & Fine Arts."

I am forever humbled to know that for our outreach efforts to other religions and denominations, I was conferred with the Martin Luther King, Jr. Award for Exemplary Community Service, presented by the NAACP "to one who cares for all persons, regardless of their race, color, or creed; to one who is a genuinely caring human being [...] a person who has been instrumental in opening paths to improve the quality of life."

At the Temple, I helped organize a dynamic series of Adult Education programs, art exhibits, unique initiatives for the men, women and children, outreach to neighbouring Jewish and non-Jewish communities, refurbishment of the building including the chapel, office and a bridal chamber, restocking the library, producing a film festival, raising the level of participation at religious services, and hosting well-attended thematic Shabbat dinners, in addition to the hundreds of daily responsibilities of a full-time congregational clergy.

Upon retiring five years later to return to Vancouver, I was presented with an Official Mayoral Citation and a Key to the City. Medford is one of America's earliest settlements, founded in 1630 and incorporated as a City in 1892; it was on Paul Revere's route as he rode through the town and alerted the militia that "The British are coming!" The synagogue also arranged for me to be awarded a Certificate of Recognition from the Massachusetts House of Representatives along with an Official Citation from the Massachusetts State Senate and presentation of the State Flag. The citation was signed by, among others, William M. Bulger, President of the Senate and brother of James J. "Whitey" Bulger Jr., an organized crime boss who, for a while, was on the FBI's "Ten Most Wanted Fugitives" list. He was considered the most wanted person on the infamous list only behind Osama bin Laden. Whitey led the Winter Hill Gang in Somerville, a neighbouring suburb. One brother was good and the other went bad. A modern-day recapitulation of the biblical story of Cain and Abel.

Elie Wiesel, Boston University

While simultaneously serving as a congregational rabbi at Temple Shalom, I was accepted into Boston University's interdisciplinary University Professors Program as a University Scholar, "a distinction awarded to a select group of students with exceptional academic achievements." I remained a doctoral student for the next five years from 1986 to 1991, four of which were as a teaching assistant for Elie Wiesel (1928–2016), who became one of the most influential mentors in my life.

Professor Herbert Mason (1932–2017) was assigned as my academic advisor. He was a wonderful man of wide interests including ancient near east civilizations, Arabic and French translation, Islamic mysticism, as well as Irish and various world literatures and mythologies. He was also a St. Louis Cardinals baseball fan, a poet and someone who understood the classical relationship between guide and disciple, teacher and friend on the path. A professor of History and Religion at Boston University, Mason was an award-winning translator of *The Epic of Gilgamesh: A Verse Narrative* (nominated for the National Book Award in 1971) and of his master teacher Louis Massignon's *Passion d'al-Halaj* for the celebrated Bollingen Series that published the entire works, in English, of Carl Jung and of other seminal European thinkers of the early twentieth century.

To illustrate the respect shown to poetry in other parts of the world, Professor Mason once shared with me an incredible story that probably took place in the late 1960s or early 1970s when he was visiting Iraq to further his primary academic research. As he was crossing the country on a train, it gradually slowed down and then came to a stop before reaching its destination at the next town. Curious, he looked out the window and saw hundreds of people crowding the tracks. He arose, walked to the platform between the carriages and asked someone what was happening. The person excitedly reported that the people heard there was a poet aboard and they came out to greet him, to hear him recite his poetry.

Herb (as he asked me to call him after I graduated) wondered who the poet might be until he was surrounded and celebrated by a group of people who discovered that *he* was the poet, the translator of the great *Epic of Gilgamesh.* I cry whenever I think of this story. It took thousands of years for a culture to learn to appreciate poetry to such an extent. If only there weren't wars; then poetry and its sister arts could inspire the world.

The faculty of the University Professors Program built their own intellectual bridges between various disciplines of the humanities, social sciences and natural sciences. The faculty included some of the most distinguished scholars at Boston University, featuring Nobel Prize laureates in Literature, Peace and Physics, MacArthur Fellows, and members of international academies. Most significant for me was Professor Elie Wiesel, Auschwitz survivor, living memorial, and Nobel Laureate for Peace. As one of his teaching assistants, while also studying literature and religion, I came to better appreciate the realities of history, the twin angels of Life and Death, the face of kindness and the shadow of evil, communal responsibilities and having a family of my own.

I learned so much from Elie Wiesel but a short list will have to suffice for now.

- *The Essential vs the Trivial:* I once told him that I wanted to know everything, to absorb all knowledge. When faced with two hundred magazine titles in a subway newsstand, for example, I wanted to pour all their contents into my hungry heart. But if I did so, I might also be wasting time and engaging in non-essential information. He paused for a moment and uttered only two Hebrew words:

Ikar ve'tofel. Translated as "primary and secondary," it is a principle that discusses the tension between the Essential vs the Trivial. He was advising me to be more discriminating, to keep my attention on that which was most important and not to be distracted by all the rest.

• *The importance of music,* of sound and rhythm in life, writing and teaching.

• The significance of both of us belonging to *Shevet Levi,* the biblical tribe of Levi, the tribe of teachers and how seriously he took his responsibility as a teacher.

• *How everything I needed to know could be communicated without uttering a word:* I learned this during one of my private meetings with him. Cognizant of the preciousness of his time, I didn't want to waste it with foolish questions or with something that I could probably figure out myself. I entered his office, sat on the couch opposite his chair, and suddenly experienced a wave of silent answers to my every query. After a few short moments, I arose, thanked him and left. It was a lesson in self-sufficiency forged in the crucible of respect.

• *Self-worth and a fair wage:* Besides being offered scholarships, teaching assistants were also paid a basic stipend. Because I was a foreign student working in an American university, I had to apply for a special visa before I could be paid. The bureaucracy, however, was so difficult to navigate that I decided not to apply. When Prof. Wiesel asked me about it one day, I told him, somewhat altruistically, that just studying with him was reward enough. I was surprised by his reaction which was insistent that I follow through with the visa and get paid a fair wage. Once again, labour laws and respect for the worker as described in the Torah had won over the day. I've applied that principle numerous times since then: many have benefitted.

• *Do not presume to speak for others—let authenticity speak its own mind:* Whenever we studied the literature of another culture or religion, it was not enough that we spoke about it in a second-hand abstract manner. Wiesel made sure that we invited a practitioner of that tradition as a guest resource to educate the class and engage in conversation.

• *Belief and blessings; wrestling and conversations with God.*

• *We are living in an age of biblical proportions:* In order to impress upon us the significance of the historical moment and the role each of us can play within it, he described our age—the past one hundred years—as one of biblical proportions.

Prof. Wiesel was a disciplined but gentle mentor and an exacting but poetic thinker. He encouraged us to "think higher and feel deeper." The Talmud (*Sanhedrin* 37a) describes each individual as an entire world, so whether we take responsibility only for ourselves or for the entire planet, we are all responsible for a kind of global civilization.

Other comments he made that have remained with me include:

• "For the dead and the living, we must bear witness."

• "Human suffering anywhere concerns men and women everywhere."

• "The opposite of love is not hate, it's indifference. The opposite of art is not ugliness, it's indifference. The opposite of faith is not heresy, it's indifference."

Prof. Wiesel introduced me to literature as I had never known it before. He perceived it from the inside, in an intimate sort of way, because he wrote as the masters did and lived it all the more. His diligence, strength and humility, as much as his wide knowledge and firsthand experience with both the suffering and nobility of humanity, forged him into a unique individual and an inspiring ambassador.

My dissertation at Boston University—titled *Two Trees Planted in the Midst of an Enigmatic Garden: A Four-Dimensional Study of a Neglected*

Archetype of Centre as Suggested by Genesis 2:8-9—was a multilevel investigation into the Tree of Life and the Tree of the Knowledge of Good & Evil planted in the centre of the Garden of Eden. It focused on a critical commentary of the original biblical text, a critique of its literature, a chapter dedicated to comparative religions and mythologies, and with another chapter on asymmetry in sacred geography as a neglected archetype of centre.

The concluding section of the dissertation (written during late night sessions when I couldn't concentrate on anything else, my eyes half closed, slumped in the chair with my nose about level with the desk) was a creative narrative imagining a return to the paradise from which we were exiled. Lost in the mists of time, protected by disbelief, fierce guardian Angels of Destruction and swiftly spinning Swords of Fire, the urge to be reunited with the Ideal is part of the eternal journey upon which we all set out but never quite arrive. The work was awarded the University Professors Alumni Award for the year's outstanding dissertation.

Inspired by these aforementioned teachers and guides, I was gradually becoming brave enough to accept my own thoughts.

Psychogeography:
Mutual Influence of Cosmology and Human Geography

Over the years, I came to realize that the various places in which I lived affected me in subtle but powerful ways. This was part of the discipline of *human geography* that studied how our species affects the planet and how natural phenomena shapes us in return; how we react differently if living by a river or a desert, at the foot of a mountain or deep in a valley; how the winds sculpt us and the rains irrigate our bodies; how the heat forms our character and the seasons conduct the rhythm of our deeds.

Ancient and Medieval philosophies worldwide had long ago observed another structural correspondence: that between the macrocosm and the microcosm. William Blake eloquently expressed this sentiment in his *Auguries of Innocence* from 1803:

> *To see a World in a Grain of Sand*
> *And a Heaven in a Wild Flower*
> *Hold Infinity in the palm of your hand*
> *And Eternity in an hour*

This Blakean view posits that the nature of the greater cosmos can be inferred by observing truths about the lesser cosmos, and vice versa. The ancient Hermetic teaching declares: "As Above, so Below," meaning "That which is Below corresponds to that which is Above, and that which is Above corresponds to that which is Below, to accomplish the Miracle of the One Thing."

The corresponding analogies provided a map of the universe, a divine cartography, and impregnated the universe with meaning. Since it was believed that nothing could exist without the fiat of God, everything was considered to have various types of a soul—whether rocks or waters, vegetation, animals, humans or non-corporeal forces.

Functions of the Seven Classical Planets (Moon, Mercury, Venus, Sun, Mars, Jupiter and Saturn) were seen as comparable to the physiological functions of human organs. The Moon, for example, was associated with water and kidneys; the Sun with fire and heart; Jupiter with air and liver; Saturn with earth and spleen.

Various theories arose throughout history that offered further correspondences mirroring the macrocosm and the microcosm. Every part of the human body was compared to aspects of the world: The right eye represents the Sun; the left eye, the Moon; the circulation of blood and other bodily fluids are similar to the rivers, lakes and oceans; the hair on our bodies is analogous to trees and other vegetation that covers the Earth; our lungs are the winds, while our bones represent the rocky mantle and minerals.

The Jewish Andalusian poet and philosopher Solomon Ibn Gabirol (1021–1058 [or 1070?] CE) noted in his *Mekor Hayim* 3:44: "If you want to form an idea of the construction of the universe, you only have to observe the construction of the human body, in which you may find an analogy."

Such is the vehicle of correspondences, a theoretical principle extending throughout the universe. It was Job, in his suffering, who was finally able to declare: "Through [observing] my body I will see God! I will see him for myself. I will see him with my own eyes; I and not a stranger. I am overwhelmed at the thought!" (Job 19:26–27).

In my search for meaning and explorations into the distant shores of understanding, the world became my laboratory, the universe my companion. I learned to relate to primary texts and yearn for *direct encounters* with nature. Reading about anything second-hand became less interesting: such mediated knowledge may have served as an introduction but ultimately it created a barrier between the phenomena in which I was interested and myself.

Just as Zeus gave birth to Athena fully formed from his head, so creative thoughts and inventive ideas came cascading out of my uterus-like mind. That way, my increasingly original thoughts, words and actions became more personal. I nurtured them like children and took responsibility for their maturation in the family of applied ideas. I learned the unspoken names of each previously unborn concept, and was sometimes also gifted with the unique language that each spirited concept transported from the dark, velvet recesses of their concealed gestation.

A virtual menagerie of information, knowledge and wisdom still dwells in the fertile Garden of All Origins awaiting our discovery. Each one, every species of thought, each burst of imagination, expresses itself in its own way. Only the limitations of human arrogance and a wounded sense of self (remnants of exiled separation from the Four-headed River flowing from beneath the Trees of Life and Knowledge) stand in the way of mutual understanding.

We are informed that some individuals, such as the Baal Shem Tov and King Solomon, returned to the metaphysical Garden where they were able to commune with nature. Solomon, in his wisdom, "knew all about plants, from the [huge] cedar in Lebanon to the [tiny] hyssop that sprouts in the cracks of a wall. He understood everything about animals and birds, reptiles and fish" (1 Kings 4:29-34). This, too, is Moses' prayer for universal prophecy when he implored: "I wish that all the Lord's people were prophets and that the Lord would put his Spirit upon them!" (Numbers 11:29). The vision was later reiterated by both Habakkuk (2:14) and Isaiah: "They shall not hurt or destroy in all my holy mountain; for the earth shall be full of knowledge [...] as the waters cover the sea (Isaiah 11:9).

Our technologically saturated generation is approaching the point of universal knowledge but two questions remain: what is the content of that knowledge and what do we do with it?

Whether there is a named god of cosmic history inexorably guiding the universe in a particular eschatological direction, or an atheistic source of accidental phenomena, it still seems that there is meaning in the moment and that each of our thoughts, words and actions make a difference, be it ever so subtle or terribly significant. Carl Jung notes this sensation, among many other mystical imaginings, in his *Red Book: Liber Novus*, a folio manuscript composed between 1914 and 1917, but which was not formally published until 2009:

"My soul, where are you? Do you hear me? I speak.
I call you—are you there? I have returned.
I am here again. I have shaken the dust
of all the lands from my feet, and
I have come to you
again."

Night of the Cabbalist, Meron, Israel, 1935, by Nachum Tim Gidal, and featured on the cover of Gidal: The Unusual Friendship of Yosef Wosk and Tim Gidal, Letters and Photos (D&M 2022).

AFTERWORD

A Cosmic Footnote to an Imperfect Life

"We are stardust, we are golden." – Joni Mitchell

WE ARE AS OLD AS THE UNIVERSE and fellow travellers upon its many paths of inexorable unfolding. In a more local sense, we are all descendants of the formation of the earth about 4.5 billion years ago: she really is Mother Earth. Some religious traditions such as the Bible and the Koran, when taken literally (although most adherents also interpret parts of them symbolically), describe a world that is less than 6,000 years old, while, at the other end of the time-bound spectrum, current scientific theories date the birth of the universe itself to about 13.8 billion years ago. A few astrophysicists suggest it may be even twice as old as that. A Hindu Vedic text calculates that the cosmos is over 155 trillion human years old and that its total life span will be 311 trillion years. When it comes to such matters, perhaps the best strategy is to remember that these estimates are all theories based upon the most recent scientific knowledge or interpretations of scriptures. Like an unbiased child in the playground of life, I find it most advantageous to keep our opinions fluid and open to rapidly advancing discoveries.

The website *Universe Today: Space and Astronomy News* has summarized human development according to the following timeline:

"While our ancestors have been around for about six million years, the modern form of humans only evolved about 200,000 years ago. Civilization as we know it is only about 6,000 years old, and industrialization started in earnest only in the 1800s."

I was born in the Spring of 1949, not even a footnote to human history, let alone to geologic, galactic or universal chronology. I was fortunate to be born in a peaceful country with one of the highest standards of living in the world; lucky to be born after the Holocaust and not to have been slaughtered in the poison of its tortured shadow; and privileged to receive a good education and advanced healthcare.

But, like many of us, I have struggled for all the rest, grappling with a sense of self, creative direction, completing what seemed like impossible tasks, coping with the discipline of work and responsibilities, dealing with addictive reactions to stress, and wrestling with emotional trauma from centuries of persecution.

I was always serious and dedicated to fulfilling what I could, and yet I often felt inadequate to the challenges at hand. I stumbled as much as strode; ruined as much as repaired; made as many mistakes in thought, emotion and action as I was able to bring about good, even noble, results.

I am an imperfect messenger who learned from imperfect teachers. No more; no less. Much information was encoded at birth, the gift of evolutionary biology; the rest was gleaned from personal observations and from interactions with family, friends and teachers—whether human or in a multitude of other guises. My intentions have been sincere and my efforts diligent even if I was occasionally led astray by other aspects of human consciousness such as an overbearing ego, mistaken logic, bruised emotions, misguided actions and sexual desires. The "weakness" is all mine as are errors in judgment and occasional subtle manipulation for personal gain.

Part of the source of our conflicted personalities is that we are not just the product of a unidimensional singular brain but are rather a complex conglomeration of multiple lobes, a bouquet brain composed of six main parts—the frontal lobe, parietal lobe, brain stem, temporal lobe, cerebellum and occipital lobe—further divided into two hemispheres, the right and left brains. The number of synapses in the brain is estimated to be a quadrillion and each one contains different molecular switches. According to theoretical physicist Michio Kaku, "the human brain is the most complicated object in the known universe". We are usually able to successfully orchestrate consciousness among its many instruments but, not infrequently, one of the other brain identities rears its needy head and demands attention. During such temporary episodes, and especially if one suffers from ongoing mental health issues, we really are "out of our minds".

When I review the sweep of my life, it seems more like a dream than reality. So much of what I've written about here, in this publication, feels like the fading echo of a distant memory. All was interesting or even necessary at the time but now they are merely lettered scratches on recycled paper.

Beyond ego and self, and with what remains of the embers of my mind, I would still like to embrace omniscience, omnipotence and omnipresence. Not because they are mountains to climb or goals to achieve—so far, no one has ever attained them—but because they exemplify the Bible's first description of humanity: "Created in the image of God; male and female they were created" (although some may cleverly reverse the ancient formula to read: "People created deities in their image; gods and goddesses they were created").

(Do not be put off by the word "God"; it is only one of many awkward attempts to name the Ineffable in both its immanent manifestation and hidden presence.) If the transcendent deity is all-knowing, ever-able and ever-present, then we, too, evolved as we are in the spiritual image of the Essence of All, should be able to inhabit such principles.

Whether you are religious, agnostic or atheist, it does not matter. The attributes of knowledge, presence and power are not just part of a sacred narrative but are an observation into, and a description of, the intrinsic nature of human consciousness. They are signposts along the road leading towards a viable awakening of the possible human. We are not merely separate from the universe—though a significant characteristic of our consciousness thrives on identifying "the other"— nor are we simply a thread in its expansive fabric, but we are the universe, the cosmos made conscious of itself.

Some believe that this one life is not enough to contain the immortal soul. Although our physical lives may end, they believe our souls continue their journeys after death into the World to Come, followed by some form of reincarnation back into this world.

When walking with my father through a cemetery many years ago, I asked him if he thought there was a *Yenne Velt* (another World to Come). He responded: "No. This is all there is. This is all we get." Later, as we paused in front of the headstone of a friend, he quipped: "I know more people in here than out there."

Various religious doctrines envision vast realms of spirit worlds, much larger than our own—places of reward and punishment; pure heavens, cleansing purgatories and tortuous hells. Humans have long believed there must be ethereal estates such as Paradise, Garden of Eden, Jannah, Valhalla, Nirvana and countless others.

If reincarnation exists, then I must have lived and died thousands or even millions of times as my soul matured through its learning development. My various abandoned bodies were recycled by nature's efficient technologies, perfected over billions of years.

Perhaps the Persian poet, Jalal ad'Din Rumi (1207–1273), expressed it best in his poem *When Was I Less By Dying?*, translated by Arthur John Arberry:

I died as a mineral and became a plant,
I died as plant and became animal,

I died as animal and I was human.
Why should I fear? When was I less by dying?
Yet once more I shall die, to soar
With angels blest; but even from angelhood
I must pass on: all except God perishes.
Only when I have given up my angel-soul,
Shall I become what no mind has ever conceived.
Oh, let me not exist! for Non-existence
Proclaims in organ tones, To God we shall return.

But if reincarnation does not exist, then this is my one, unique, and unrepeatable life. Thus far I've lived my life as if it were a one-time event. Each day is filled with creative intensity, a minute or two of doubt, a smattering of despair, along with flashes of wonder and gratitude.

The end of the week is then crowned with a full Shabbat, a Sabbath night and day that anoints each seventh cycle. It recapitulates a kind of *Olam Ha'ba*, a paradisiacal afterlife in the midst of this mundane temporal existence. As the Ahad Ha'am (Asher Ginsberg, poet, philosopher, 1856–1927) once observed: "More than the Jews have kept the Sabbath, the Sabbath has kept the Jews."

I feel that even the Big Bang theory is only one in a series of rhythmic, repeatable, sensate actions and reactions, a sequence of cosmic exhalations and inhalations, and that ours is just one universe in the midst of a larger collection of such vessels that combine to form a multiverse. While each atom is equivalent to a solar system, every galaxy is but a drop of dust.

But even those narratives seem like limited descriptions of physical reality, for I wonder what was the origin of the ultra-compressed material that exploded during the conceptual Big Bang; what receptacle cradles space and what lays beyond its borders; what happened before "the beginning" and what will be the culmination of the seemingly never ending drama? While some theories suggest that time and space—or the spacetime continuum—always existed and always will, I am not comfortable with such an open-ended formula. Nothing within the universe shares such characteristics so how could the container itself be described as such?

In the world of metaphysics, even infinity is just another number. While respecting, caring for and needing physical reality with its accompanying *élan vital*, I am more interested in what kabbalists refer to as the *Ain Ain Sof*, the Origin of Origins, where nothing, not even your next questioning thought, exits. It lays beyond all veils: words armed with metaphors cannot describe it nor can poetry penetrate its illusions. Words and logic, like sight and sound, are limited by their physical properties; even silence is sound in such a transcendent "realm". I often feel the presence of this noncorporeal, unmanifest Essence. Imagination may be able to visit for a second or two but madness, or death, is often the price of an extended stay.

We are a rather unique recipe of stardust and other interstellar ingredients, a product of the Kosmic Kitchen who can trace our genesis back to the emergence of creation itself. We are the offspring of a trillion unions and just as many decays. Each of us was born from a matrix of nearly impossible odds; we almost didn't exist but do, temporarily, for now. We have battled—as has any element that desires to preserve its individuated presence in the face of opposing forces—but have also been the heir of magnificent benefits and witnessed astonishing wonders.

Humbled by my encounters with the Ways of the World, I go, now, for a walk in the Garden of Earthly Delights in the afternoon of what has been a long and everlasting day. A gentle breeze caresses what's left of the Edenic ideal where dandelion seeds are scattered like exploding stars in the crucible of celestial space. It is as Rabindrath Tagore intoned in *The Gardener*:

Much knowing has turned my hair grey,
and much watching has made my sight dim.
For years I have gathered and heaped up
scraps and fragments of things. . .

I let go my pride of learning and judgment of right and of wrong.
I'll shatter memory's vessel, scattering the last drop of tears.
With the foam of the berry-red wine
I will bathe and brighten my laughter. . .
I'll take the holy vow
to be worthless,
to be drunken
and go
to the
dogs.

ABOUT YOSEF WOSK

PREVIOUSLY INVOLVED IN THE publication of books pertaining to psychology, theology, poetry, photography, food, pedagogy and art, Yosef Wosk provided the Afterword to *Out of Hiding: The Holocaust Literature of British Columbia* (Ronsdale Press 2022), winner of the George Ryga Award for Social Awareness, and his correspondence was the main component of *GIDAL: The Unusual Friendship of Yosef Wosk and Tim Gidal* (Douglas & McIntyre 2022), winner of the Pinsky Givon Non-Fiction Prize for the Western Canada Jewish Book Awards.

An Officer of the *Order of Canada*, a member of the Order of British Columbia and a rare recipient of *Freedom of the City* from the City of Vancouver, Yosef Wosk developed the *Philosophers' Café* as one of the largest conversation café programs in the world, attracting more than 110,000 participants since 1998. Having served as a Shadbolt Fellow, Simons Fellow, Adjunct Professor in the Department of Humanities and Director of Interdisciplinary Programs in Continuing Studies at Simon Fraser University, he also gave rise to the *Canadian Academy of Independent Scholars*.

In addition to being an ordained rabbi (Yeshiva University) and receiving two honorary doctorates, Yosef Wosk holds Ph.Ds in Religion & Literature (Boston University) as well as in Psychology, and masters degrees in Education (Yeshiva) and Theology (Harvard). He has founded hundreds of libraries on all seven continents, supported museums worldwide and endowed Vancouver's Poet Laureate program. Cited by the *Vancouver Sun* as one of the top ten thinkers of British Columbia, he remains active as an art collector and a public speaker.

He lives in Vancouver, in close contact with his three adult children. For more, see yosefwosk.org.